画儿上的美人

The Lady in the Painting

画儿上的美人

The Lady in the Painting

A Basic Chinese Reader
Expanded Edition
by Claudia Ross with Jocelyn Ross

Story by Fred Fang-yü Wang

Drawings by Luke Chen

Simplified Characters

Yale UNIVERSITY PRESS/NEW HAVEN & LONDON

First edition published 1957. Pinyin Romanization added in 1983.

Publisher: Mary Jane Peluso
Project Editor: Timothy Shea
Manuscript Editor: Jack Borrebach
Production Editor: Ann-Marie Imbornoni
Production Controller: Maureen Noonan

Printed in the United States of America.

Library of Congress Control Number: 2007936891

ISBN 978-0-300-11549-9 (paperback [traditional char] : alk. paper)

ISBN 978-0-300-21448-2 (paperback [simplified char])

A catalogue record for this book is available from the British Library.

10 9 8 7 6 5 4 3 2 1

Contents

目录 mùlù

Acknowledgments

First and foremost, we wish to thank John Montanaro, the editor of the former Far Eastern Publications, for his assistance and encouragement in the development of this expanded edition. Though an editor for many years, John is at heart and at profession a teacher, and it is his love of teaching Chinese and his dedication to the field that inspired us to work on this project.

We thank Anne Shu-qing Guo for her careful proofreading of many earlier versions of this text, and Steven Katsos, Holly Hunt, and Joel Villa for their technical assistance. We thank Galal Walker, Dana Scott Bourgerie, Zhenjun Zhang, and Jen-Mei Ma for their many helpful observations and suggestions as they reviewed the working manuscript of this book.

Finally, we thank the editors of Yale University Press for all of their assistance in the review and production of this book. All errors are our own.

Introduction

This book is an expanded edition of the story The Lady in the Painting, written in the style of a Chinese folktale by Fred Fang-yü Wang and richly illustrated with drawings by Luke Chen. First published in 1957 by Far Eastern Publications, it continues to charm Chinese language learners and to motivate them to continue to study Chinese.

The story is told with vocabulary and structures familiar to students who have completed a basic course in Mandarin Chinese. Using an inventory of only about 300 Chinese characters, it serves as an excellent transition between the short reading passages that students encounter in a basic level Chinese course and the longer and more demanding passages in subsequent levels. At the same time, it reinforces the structures and vocabulary introduced in the basic level course and provides a rich context for classroom discussion in Chinese.

This expanded edition preserves the original story in all of its features and adds resources that turn the story into a vehicle for the development of oral and written communication skills in Chinese. Each of the eight chapters of the book includes an expanded vocabulary list, structure notes and exercises, and reading comprehension questions. Chapters 4–8 include narrative practice exercises which challenge students to use targeted vocabulary and grammatical structures to write extended narratives on specific themes.

This expanded edition of The Lady in the Painting can be used as the primary textbook for a low-intermediate class or as a supplementary text. Depending upon the reading proficiency of the students and the expectations of the teacher, it can be completed in as little as a few weeks or as long as a semester. The many resources that accompany the story also make the book adaptable for self-study for low-intermediate students.

This book uses pinyin Romanization and follows the orthographic conventions outlined in the Basic Rules for Hanyu Pinyin Orthography by the Commission for Pinyin Orthography of the P.R.C. as presented in the ABC Chinese-English Dictionary (John DeFrancis, ed.), with one exception. To guide learners in their pronunciation, tone changes that occur within the boundary of a single word are written into the pinyin tone spelling of the word. Thus, for example, the pinyin spelling of 不但 is presented here as búdàn and not as bùdàn. 所以 is presented as suóyǐ and not as the unchanged suǒyǐ. ABC Chinese-English Dictionary is used as the reference for grammatical category labels and English translations.

Abbreviations of Grammatical Terms

ADV	*Adverb*	ADV P	*Adverbial Phrase*
AV	*Adjectival Verb*	AVP	*Adjectival Verb Phrase*
C	*Connecting Word*		
DIR	*Directional Word*		
INT	*Intensifier*		
LOC	*Locative Particle*		
M	*Measure*		
MV	*Modal Verb*	MVP	*Modal Verb Phrase*
N	*Noun*	NP	*Noun Phrase*
NEG	*Negation*		
P	*Preposition*	PP	*Prepositional Phrase*
PrN	*Pronoun*		
RV	*Resultative Verb*	RVP	*Resultative Verb Phrase*
S	*Sentence*		
SP	*Specifier*		
V	*Verb*	VP	*Verb Phrase*
VO	*Verb + Object*		

第一章：张大明

从前有一个人，姓张，叫大明。他没有哥哥，没有弟弟。父亲母亲也都过去了。家里就是他一个人。也没有钱。他已经三十多岁了，还没有太太，当然也没有孩子。他每天早上出去做工，晚上回家。

他的家在城外头。离做工的地方不远，他每天早上，在路上看看山，看看水，也有时候唱唱歌儿。

他有不少朋友，朋友们都很喜欢他。他们天天在一块儿做工，也在一块儿玩儿。他们真是「做工的时候做工，玩儿的时候玩儿」。所以他们都很高兴。可是到了晚上，别人都回家了，张大明也回家了。别人家里有太太，有孩子。太太做饭的时候，他们可以跟孩子玩儿。可是张大明回到家里，什么人都没有，饭得自己做，家里的事情也得自己做。想跟人说话，可是没有人听。所以有时候他自己跟自己说话。

他有一个朋友，是一位老先生。这位老先生姓高，人都叫他高老先生。这位老先生会画画儿，画得好极了。很有名。他常画山水，也会画人，可是不常画。

高老先生看张大明家里没有太太，没有孩子。一个人在家里一定很没意思。所以就想画一张画儿，送给他。他给张大明画了一张很好看的美人。他画那张画儿的时候常想，张大明的屋子里有这样一张画儿，也许他晚上回家以后，可以觉得家里有一个人。他把画儿画完了，就叫张大明到他家来拿。有几个人跟张大明一块儿来看那张画儿。

他们都是张大明的朋友，有一个认识高老先生的，就跟张大明一块儿进去了。还有几个人，不认识高老先生，就站在门外头看。他们都说画得真好。高老先生看见他们都喜欢他画的画儿，他也很高兴。

张大明谢了谢高老先生，拿着画儿就回家了。

张大明有了这张画儿以后，他早上起来就跟画上的人说，「早。」出去做工的时候，就跟她说，「再见。」他做完了工，晚上回来，就坐下看那张画儿。家里的事情都不愿意做了。不但有时候忘了做饭，也有时候把吃饭都忘了。

有一天，他又忘了做饭了。没吃饭就去睡觉去了。可是怎么睡也睡不着。他没法子，就起来做一点儿点心吃。吃着东西，也看那张画儿。还跟那个画儿上的人说，「明天你给我做饭，好不好？」

第二天早上，他出去做工以前，拿了一块昨天夜里做的点心，笑着跟画儿上的人说，别忘了给我做饭。我五点多钟回来。再见。

那个时候，正是七八月，是最忙的时候。所以那天他在外头应当做的事情很多。

到了五点多钟，他正要回家的时候，有一个朋友跑来说，「老张，你能不能帮我一点儿忙？」老张说，「什么事？」

那个人的太太病了。得到城里头去请大夫。可是家里没人能去，所以要请张大明帮忙，问张大明能去不能。张大明最愿意帮朋友忙，所以他听见这个话就立刻到城里头去了。

他把大夫请来，回家的时候，在路上看见家里房子上头有很多烟。他心里觉得奇怪极了。他怕是昨天晚上做点心的时候，火还着着，也许房子里着火了。所以他立刻就往家跑，想去看看怎么回事。

他跑到家，开开门，往屋子里一看，你想屋子里着了火没有？

他跑到屋子里一看，屋子里没着火，他就放心了。再一看火上有做好了的吃的东西。他觉得奇怪极了。他想，这是谁做的呢？他看了看那张画儿。他又想，真是画儿上的那个人给我做的吗？可是画儿上的人，怎么能下来呢？他想来想去，想不出来是怎么回事。

后来他把吃的拿出来放在桌子上，坐下就吃。真好吃。一吃东西，什么都忘了。什么都不想了。不大的工夫，把所有的东西都吃完了。吃完了，他就坐在那儿看着画儿上的人，笑着跟她说，「饭真是你做的吗？做得真好。谢谢，谢谢。」画儿上的人没说什么。

张大明睡了一夜觉，第二天早上还是想昨天那件奇怪的事。他想也许是朋友们跟他开玩笑。他们来给他做了饭就走了。叫他觉得奇怪。可是是谁呢？对了，老王爱开玩笑，可是他不会做饭。也许他跟他太太一块儿来的，是他太太做的饭。做好了饭，放在那儿，就走了。他又想，不对，不对。王太太是会做饭，可是她平常做的饭，我吃过，没有这么好吃。这是谁呢？

他想来想去，还是不知道是怎么回事。最后，他想他得去做工去了，他又看了看那张画儿，笑着跟画儿上的人说，要是你能下来做饭，今天还请你给我做。不但请你做饭，你看，我的衣裳坏了，我还要请你给我缝一缝衣裳。你看着，我放在这儿了。谢谢你，别忘了。他说完了，就走了。

Chapter 1 Vocabulary

画(儿)	huà(r)	*N*	*painting(s), picture(s)*
美人	měirén	*N*	*beautiful person*
章	zhāng	*N*	*chapter*
从前	cóngqián	*ADV*	*in the past, once upon a time*
叫	jiào	*V*	*be called*
哥哥	gēge	*N*	*older brother*
弟弟	dìdi	*N*	*younger brother*
父亲	fùqin	*N*	*father*
母亲	mǔqin	*N*	*mother*
过去了	guòqule	*V*	*passed away (died)*
岁	suì	*M*	*years of age*
当然	dāngrán	*ADV*	*of course*
孩子	háizi	*N*	*child*
早上	zǎoshang	*N*	*morning*
做工	zuò gōng	*VP (VO)*	*work (do work)*
晚上	wǎnshang	*N*	*evening*
回	huí	*V*	*return (to a place)*
回家	huí jiā	*VP (VO)*	*return home*
唱	chàng	*V*	*sing*
歌(儿)	gē(r)	*N*	*song, songs*
唱歌(儿)	chàng gē(r)	*VP (VO)*	*sing a song (songs)*
不少	bù shǎo	*NEG + AV*	*a lot (not few)*

一块(儿)	yíkuài (yíkuàr)	*ADV*	*together*
玩(儿)	wán (wár)	*V*	*have fun (play)*
所以	suóyǐ	*C*	*therefore*
高兴	gāoxìng	*AV*	*happy*
别人	bié rén	*NP*	*other people*
得	děi	*MV*	*must*
自己	zìjǐ	*PrN*	*(by) oneself*
跟	gēn	*P*	*with*
听	tīng	*V*	*listen*
有时候	yǒu shíhou	*ADV*	*sometimes*
位	wèi	*M*	*M for people (polite)*
叫	jiào	*V*	*call (someone something)*
画	huà	*V*	*paint*
画画(儿)	huà huà(r)	*VP (VO)*	*paint picture(s)*
有名	yǒu míng	*AVP*	*famous*
常	cháng	*ADV*	*often*
山水	shānshuǐ	*N*	*landscapes, scenery*
没意思	méi yìsi	*NEG + AVP*	*not interesting*
有意思	yǒu yìsi	*AVP (VO)*	*interesting*
送	sòng	*V*	*send, present as a gift*
屋子	wūzi	*N*	*room*
这样	zhèyàng	*SP + M*	*this kind of*
也许	yéxǔ	*ADV*	*perhaps*

觉得	juéde	*V*	*think, feel*
认识	rènshi	*V*	*know (a person)*
进去	jìnqu	*V + DIR*	*enter*
站	zhàn	*V*	*stand*
起来	qǐlai	*V + DIR*	*get up*
出去	chūqu	*V + DIR*	*go out*
坐下	zuòxia	*V + DIR*	*sit down*
愿意	yuànyi	*AV*	*willing*
不但	búdàn	*C*	*not only*
睡觉	shuì jiào	*VP (VO)*	*sleep*
睡不着	shuìbuzháo	*RV*	*unable to fall asleep*
点心	diǎnxīn	*N*	*snack*
东西	dōngxi	*N*	*thing (concrete, not abstract)*
夜里	yè lǐ	*N + LOC*	*in the night*
笑	xiào	*V*	*smile*
别	bié	*NEG*	*don't*
应当	yīngdāng	*MV*	*should*
事情	shìqing	*N*	*thing (abstract, e.g. work)*
正要	zhèng yào	*ADV + MV*	*be just about to*
帮忙	bāng máng	*VP (VO)*	*help*
帮我一点忙	bāng wǒ yīdiǎn máng	*VP*	*help me a bit*
病	bìng	*V*	*sick*
大夫	dàifu	*N*	*doctor*

立刻	lìkè	*ADV*	*immediately*
烟	yān	*N*	*smoke*
心里	xīn lǐ	*N + LOC*	*in his heart*
奇怪	qíguài	*AV*	*strange*
怕	pà	*V*	*fear*
火	huǒ	*N*	*fire*
着	zháo	*V*	*burn*
着火	zháo huǒ	*VP (VO)*	*catch on fire*
往	wǎng	*P*	*toward*
跑	pǎo	*V*	*run*
怎么回事？	zěnme huí shì?	*Question*	*what is going on?*
开	kāi	*V*	*open*
放心	fàng xīn	*VP (VO)*	*relax, stop worrying*
下来	xiàlai	*V + DIR*	*come down*
想来想去	xiǎnglái xiǎngqù	*V + DIR*	*think over and over*
后来	hòulái	*ADV*	*afterwards*
拿	ná	*V*	*take*
放	fàng	*V*	*put down*
桌子	zhuōzi	*N*	*table*
不大的工夫	bù dà de gōngfu	*ADV P*	*in a short time*
开玩笑	kāi wánxiào	*VP (VO)*	*play a joke*
叫	jiào	*V*	*cause (someone to do or feel something)*
爱	ài	*V*	*love*

平常	píngcháng	*ADV*	*usually*
这么好吃	zhème hǎo chī	*ADV + VP*	*this good to eat, so good to eat*
衣裳	yīshang	*N*	*clothing*
坏	huài	*AV*	*torn, broken, ruined*
缝	féng	*V*	*sew*

Chapter 1 Structure Notes

1.1 Appositive Noun Phrases

A noun or pronoun may be followed by another noun phrase that provides additional information about the noun. The second noun phrase often includes a number and measure.

> 家里就是<u>他</u>[一个人]。
> Jiā lǐ jiù shì <u>tā</u> [yī gè ré<u>n</u>].
> *In his family there was only <u>him</u> [one person].*

1.2. Verb repetition

> 他每天早上，在路上<u>看看</u>山，<u>看看</u>水，也有时候<u>唱唱</u>歌儿。
> Tā měitiān zǎoshang, zài lùshang <u>kàn kàn</u> shān, <u>kàn kàn</u> shuǐ, yě yǒu shíhou <u>chàng chàng</u> gēr.
> *Every morning on the road he <u>looked</u> at the mountains and he <u>looked</u> at the water, and sometimes he <u>sang</u>.*

Verbs that refer to activities may be repeated, as in this sentence from Chapter 1. Repetition conveys the sense that these activities are casually done and are not performed in order to accomplish some specific goal or task.

1.3. 的时候 de shíhou *while, when*

的时候 de shíhou is used to indicate that two events are going on at the same time. It can be translated as *while* or *when* in English. In this sentence from Chapter 1, the two events are *painting* (画) and *thinking* (想).

> 他画那张画儿<u>的时候</u>常想，张大明的屋子里有这样一张画儿，也许他晚上回家以后，可以觉得家里有一个人。
>
> Tā huà nà zhāng huàr <u>de shíhou</u> cháng xiǎng, Zhāng Dàmíng de wūzi lǐ yǒu zhèyàng yī zhāng huàr, yéxǔ tā wǎnshang huí jiā yǐhòu, kéyǐ juéde jiā lǐ yǒu yī gè rén.
>
> *<u>When</u> he painted the picture he often thought, (if) there were this kind of picture in Zhang Daming's room, perhaps after he returned home at night he could feel that there was a person in his house.*

的时候 de shíhou occurs after the first event, <u>at the end</u> of the first clause.
In English, *while* or *when* occurs before the first event, <u>at the beginning</u> of the first clause.

In the following sentence from Chapter 1, [square brackets] illustrate the way that 的时候 de shíhou is grouped with the other words in the first clause.

[太太做饭的时候]，他们可以跟孩子玩儿。
[Tàitai zuò fàn de shíhou], tāmen kéyǐ gēn háizi wár.
[While their wives cook], they can play with the children.

的时候 de shíhou is not used as a question word. To ask **the question** *when*, use 什么时候 shénme shíhou *when (literally: what time)*. Here is a question with 什么时候 shénme shíhou followed by an answer. As with all content questions in Mandarin, the question word or phrase goes in the same place in the sentence as the answer.

Q: 你什么时候吃晚饭？
Nǐ shénme shíhou chī wǎnfàn?
When do you eat dinner?

A: 我六点钟吃晚饭。
Wǒ liùdiǎn zhōng chī wǎnfàn.
I eat dinner at six o'clock.

1.4. Prepositions

Mandarin prepositions include the following:

从	cóng	*from*	
到	dào	*to*	*Used with time expressions (9 to 5) and with verbs that involve movement to a destination (go to the park)*
在	zài	*at, on*	
给	gěi	*to, for*	*Used with verb that involve the transfer of items to or for someone (write a letter to her, buy a book for her)*
跟	gēn	*with*	
往	wǎng	*towards*	*Used with movement towards a direction (walk east) or towards a location (walk towards the park)*
对	duì	*to*	*Used with actions that do not involve movement or transfer of items (speak to her)*

Prepositions are always followed by a noun phrase. A preposition plus the following noun phrase is a *prepositional phrase*. Here is an example of a prepositional phrase.

跟孩子 gēn háizi *with (the) children*

Prepositional phrases are always associated with a verb phrase.
In Mandarin, the prepositional phrase always goes *before* the verb phrase.
In English, the prepositional phrase always goes *after* the verb phrase.

In the following examples from the story, the prepositional phrase is underlined and the verb phrase is indicated with [square brackets].

太太做饭的时候，他们可以跟孩子[玩儿]。
Tàitai zuò fàn de shíhou, tāmen kéyǐ gēn háizi [wár].
While their wives cook, they can [play] with the children.

他给张大明[画了一张很好看的美人]。
Tā gěi Zhāng Dàmíng [huà le yī zhāng hěn hǎo kàn de měi rén].
He [painted a very beautiful woman] for Zhang Daming.

In Mandarin, the expression *play a joke on someone* is expressed with the preposition 跟 gēn *with* as follows:

跟 *someone* [开玩笑]
gēn *someone* [kāi wánxiào]
[play a joke] on someone

他想也许是朋友们跟他[开玩笑]。
Tā xiǎng yéxǔ shì péngyǒumen gēn tā [kāi wánxiào].
He thought perhaps it was his friends [playing a joke] on him.

1.5. Expressing *any*, *every*, *all*, *never*, and *no (noun)*

Mandarin does not have distinct words that can be translated as *any*, *every*, *all*, *never*, and *no (noun)*. Instead, Mandarin uses content question words in particular structures to express these meanings.

Mandarin content question words include:

谁	shéi	*who*
什么	shénme	*what*
什么时候	shénme shíhou	*when*
哪儿	nǎr	*where*

Content question words are used to express *any*, *every*, and *all* when they are followed by 都 dōu or 也 yě and occur before the verb phrase. The choice of 都 dōu or 也 yě does not affect the meaning of the expression. However, when expressing *any*, *every*, and *all*, 都 dōu is more common than 也 yě.

谁都	shéi + dōu	*everyone/anyone*
谁也	shéi + yě	
什么都	shénme + dōu	*everything/anything*
什么也	shénme + yě	

什么时候都	shénme shíhou + dōu	*every time/always/anytime*
什么时候也	shénme shíhou + yě	
哪儿都	nǎr + dōu	*everywhere/anywhere*
哪儿也	nǎr + yě	

谁都喜欢张大明。
Shéi dōu xǐhuan Zhāng Dàmíng.
Everyone likes Zhang Daming.

张大明的家里什么都有。
Zhāng Dàmíng de jiā lǐ shénme dōu yǒu.
Zhang Daming's house has everything. (In Zhang Daming's house there is everything.)

张大明的朋友什么时候都唱歌。
Zhāng Dàmíng de péngyou shénme shíhou dōu chàng gē.
Zhang Daming's friends sing all the time.

高老先生哪儿都去过。
Gāo lǎo xiānsheng nǎr dōu qùguo.
Old Mr. Gao has been everywhere.

Content question words are used to express *never* and *no (noun)* when they are followed by 都 dōu or 也 yě and occur before a negated verb phrase. The choice of 都 dōu or 也 yě does not affect the meaning of the expression. However, when expressing *never* and *no*, 也 yě is more common than 都 dōu.

谁都 + NEG	shéi + dōu + NEG	*no one*
谁也 + NEG	shéi + yě + NEG	
什么都 + NEG	shénme + dōu + NEG	*nothing*
什么也 + NEG	shénme + yě + NEG	
什么时候都 + NEG	shénme shíhou + dōu + NEG	*never*
什么时候也 + NEG	shénme shíhou + yě + NEG	
哪儿都 + NEG	nǎr + dōu + NEG	*nowhere*
哪儿也 + NEG	nǎr + yě + NEG	

谁也不会做饭。
Shéi yě bù huì zuò fàn.
No one can cook.

什么都不想了。
Shénme dōu bù xiǎng le.
He didn't think about anything anymore.

什么时候也不好。
Shénme shíhou yě bù hǎo.
No time is good.

高老先生哪儿也没有去过。
Gāo lǎo xiānsheng nǎr yě méi qùguo.
Old Mr. Gao hasn't been anywhere.

Note: If the content question word is part of a larger phrase, the entire phrase occurs before 都 dōu or 也 yě and the verb. In the following sentence from the story, the content question word 什么 shénme is part of the larger phrase 什么人 shénme rén. Notice how it occurs before 都 dōu and the verb phrase 没有 méi yǒu.

可是张大明回到家里，[什么人]都没有。
Kěshì Zhāng Dàmíng huí dào jiā lǐ, [shénme rén] dōu méi yǒu.
But when Zhang Daming returned home, there was [no one] at all.

In order to convey the meaning of *any*, *every*, *all*, *never*, or *no (noun)*, the question word (or the phrase that includes it) must occur *before the verb phrase*.

This is the case when the question word is the subject of the verb:

谁都认识张大明。
Shéi dōu rènshi Zhāng Dàmíng.
Everyone knows Zhang Daming.

and when it is the object of the verb:

say this:	**not this:**
他什么电影都看过。 Tā shénme diànyǐng dōu kànguo. *He has seen every movie.*	*他都看过什么电影。 Tā dōu kànguo shénme diànyǐng.
他谁都喜欢。 Tā shéi dōu xǐhuan. *He likes everyone.*	*他都喜欢谁。 Tā dōu xǐhuan shéi.

1.6 怎么 Verb$_1$, 都/也 Verb$_2$ zěnme Verb$_1$, dōu/yě Verb$_2$

no matter how (one) does Verb$_1$, Verb$_2$

都 dōu is more common when Verb$_2$ is affirmative. 也 yě is more common when Verb$_2$ is negated or involves negation.

As this example from Chapter 1 illustrates, $Verb_2$ is often a resultative verb. (For more on resultative verbs, see Structure Note 2.2.)

怎么睡也睡不着。
Zěnme shuì yě shuìbuzháo.
No matter how he tried to sleep he couldn't sleep.

1.7. 把 bǎ

把 bǎ sentences are used to indicate what the subject does *to* or *with* the object of 把 bǎ.

他把画儿画完了，就叫大明到他家来拿。
Tā bǎ huàr huàwán le, jiù jiào Dàmíng dào tā jiā lái ná.
He finished painting the picture and told Daming to come to his house to take it.

把 bǎ sentences can often be loosely translated as:

Noun $Phrase_1$ takes Noun $Phrase_2$ and does something with it.

This sentence from Chapter 1 can be phrased in this way:

他把画儿画完了 …
Tā bǎ huàr huàwán le …
He took the picture and finished painting it …

1.8. Manner adverbials

这位老先生会画画儿，画得好极了。
Zhè wèi lǎo xiānsheng huì huà huàr, huà de hǎojíle.
This old gentleman can paint, and he paints extremely well.

To indicate how an activity is generally performed, follow the activity verb with 得 de + adjectival verb.

他画得好。
Tā huà de hǎo.
He paints well.

Usually, an intensifier (很 hěn *very*, 太 tài *too*, 真 zhēn *really*, etc.) precedes the adjectival verb:

他画得很好。
Tā huà de hěn hǎo.
He paints very well.

As illustrated in the sentence above from Chapter 1, the intensifier 极了 jíle always follows the adjectival verb: 画得好极了 huà de hǎojíle *paints extremely well.*

If the activity verb takes an object, the verb must be included twice, once before the object, and once before the manner adverbial.

[verb + object] [verb + 得 de + adjectival verb phrase]

他[画画儿] [画得很好]。
Tā [huà huàr] [huà de hěn hǎo].
He paints pictures very well.

1.9. Verb 了 le Verb *did an action briefly or quickly*

This pattern implies that the subject did the action for a short period of time.

他看了看那张画儿。
Tā kàn le kàn nà zhāng huàr.
He took a look at the picture.

1.10. 一 yī VP_1 (就 jiù) VP_2 *as soon as VP_1, VP_2*

一 VP_1 (就) VP_2	*as soon as VP_1 occurs, VP_2 occurs,* OR
yī VP_1 (jiù) VP_2	*when VP_1 occurs, VP_2 occurs,* OR *whenever VP_1 occurs, VP_2 occurs.*

一 yī before a measure indicates the number one, but 一 yī before a verb indicates sequence. 就 jiù typically occurs before the second verb phrase in this pattern, but its presence is not obligatory.

他跑到家，开开门，往屋子里一看，你想屋子里着了火没有？
Tā pǎo dào jiā, kāi kāi mén, wǎng wūzi lǐ yī kàn, nǐ xiǎng wūzi lǐ zháo le huǒ méi yǒu?
He ran home, opened the door, and when he looked into the room, what do you think? Had the room caught fire or not?

The event described in VP_1 may be only loosely connected to the event in VP_2.

他一看，没有人了。
Tā yī kàn, méi yǒu rén le.
When he looked, there wasn't anyone there anymore.

1.11. Describing a noun with a description: description + 的 de + Noun

那天他[在外头应当做的]事情很多。
Nà tiān tā [zài wàitou yīngdāng zuò de] shìqing hěn duō.
That day the things [he had to do outdoors] were numerous.
(That day, he had a lot of things he had to do outdoors.)

In Mandarin, descriptions or modifiers of the noun always occur before the noun. Specifiers (*this/that*), numbers, and measure phrases go directly before the noun:

[number + measure] + noun	[specifier + measure] + noun
[一本]书 [yī běn] shū *[one] book*	[那本]书 [nà běn] shū *[that] book*

All other modifiers are typically followed by 的 de, though 的 de is sometimes omitted.

A single noun may be described by more than one description phrase. In this case, the noun that is being described occurs once, at the end of the series of description phrases. In the following example, each description is presented in [square brackets].

> [张大明的] [很美的] 太太
> [Zhāng Dàmíng de] [hěn měi de] tàitai
> *[Zhang Daming's] [very pretty] wife*

1.12. **The verb suffix 着 zhe**

> 第二天早上，他出去做工以前，拿了一块昨天夜里做的点心，<u>笑着</u>跟画儿上的人说，别忘了给我做饭。
>
> Dì èr tiān zǎoshang, tā chūqu zuò gōng yǐqián, ná le yī kuài zuótiān yè lǐ zuò de diǎnxin, <u>xiàozhe</u> gēn huàrshàng de rén shuō, bié wàngle gěi wǒ zuò fàn.
>
> *The next morning, before he left for work, he took one of the snacks made the night before and, <u>smiling</u>, said to the person in the picture, "Don't forget to cook for me."*

着 zhe may be suffixed to any verb that describes a situation with duration. It emphasizes the duration.
When 着 zhe is suffixed to the first verb of a sequence, it also indicates that the first verb describes the background event for the second verb.

着 zhe *emphasizes duration*	着 zhe *indicates the background event*
他在吃着饭。 Tā zài chīzhe fàn. *He is eating.*	他坐着吃饭。 Tā zuòzhe chī fàn. *He is eating seated.* 张大明拿着画儿就回家了。 Zhāng Dàmíng názhe huàr jiù huí jiā le. *Zhang Daming, holding the painting, returned home.*

1.13. The verb suffix 过 guo

过 guo can serve as a suffix for any verb that refers to a repeatable action. It indicates that the action occurred at some time in the past.

> 王太太是会做饭，可是她平常做的饭我吃过，没有这么好吃。
> Wáng tàitai shì huì zuò fàn, kěshì tā píngcháng zuò de fàn wǒ chīguo, méi yǒu zhème hào chī.
> *Mrs. Wang can cook, but I've eaten the food she usually cooks, (and it) is not this delicious.*

The use of 过 guo suggests that the action is not a common occurrence for the subject. In addition, it indicates that the action was separated from the moment of speaking by some period of time. Thus, when Zhang Daming says 她平常做的饭我吃过 tā píngcháng zuò de fàn wǒ chīguo, he implies that he ate her food some time ago in the past, and that he does not regularly eat the food that she cooks.

1.14. 怎么回事 zěnme huí shì *What's going on?*

怎么回事 zěnme huí shì is a fixed expression in Chinese. Like its English translation, it can be used as a direct question to ask for an explanation of some situation. It is also used as an indirect question, as in this sentence from Chapter 1.

> 所以他立刻就往家跑，想去看看怎么回事。
> Suóyǐ tā lìkè jiù wǎng jiā pǎo, xiǎng qù kàn kàn zěnme huí shì.
> *So he ran home immediately, thinking to see what was going on.*

It commonly occurs as an indirect question after 不知道 bù zhīdao *not know* in expressions like the following:

> 他不知道是怎么回事。
> Tā bù zhīdao shì zěnme huí shì.
> *He did not know what was going on.*

1.15. 帮忙 bāng máng *help*

帮忙 bāng máng can be used to express the meaning *help* or *help a person*. To express the meaning *help*, use subject +帮忙 bāng máng.

> 她很愿意帮忙。
> Tā hěn yuànyi bāng máng.
> *She is very willing to help.*

> 他不要帮忙。
> Tā bù yào bāng máng.
> *He does not want to help.*

To express the meaning *help a person*, add the person, usually followed by 的 de, between 帮 bāng and 忙 máng.

帮 ***person*** 的 忙	bāng ***person*** de máng	*help the person*
帮 我 的 忙	bāng wǒ de máng	*help me*
帮 朋友 的 忙	bāng péngyou de máng	*help friends*
帮 张大明 的 忙	bāng Zhāng Dàmíng de máng	*help Zhang Daming*

Here is an example of the use of帮忙 bāng máng in Chapter 1.

张大明帮了朋友的忙 。
Zhāng Dàmíng bāng le péngyou de máng.
Zhang Daming helped his friends.

Chapter 1 Structure Exercises

Using the Chapter 1 *Structure Notes* as your guide, translate the Chinese sentences to English and the English sentences to Chinese. The Chinese sentences have been selected from Chapter 1.

1.1 Appositive Noun Phrases

1. In Zhang Daming's family there were only he and his wife, two people.

2. Zhang Daming thought, "Eating dinner by myself [me, one person eating dinner] is not interesting."

1.2. Verb repetition

1. 他跑到家，开开门，往屋子里看。

1.3. 的时候 de shíhou *while, when*

1. 出去做工的时候，就跟她说「再见」。

2. 到了五点多钟，他正要回家的时候，有一个朋友跑来说，「老张，你能不能帮我一点忙？」

3. When Old Mr. Gao paints paintings, he talks to himself.

4. While Zhang Daming works, he always sings songs.

1.4. Prepositions *(The preposition is underlined in each sentence.)*

1. 他<u>给</u>张大明画了一张很好看的美人。

2. 张大明有了这张画儿以后，他早上起来就<u>跟</u>画儿上的人说：「早」。

3. 别忘了<u>给</u>我做饭。

4. 他们来<u>给</u>他做了饭就走了。

5. Every day, Zhang Daming works <u>with</u> his friends.

6. Old Mr. Gao painted a picture <u>for</u> Zhang Daming.

7. The lady in the painting cooked dinner <u>for</u> Zhang Daming.

8. Zhang Daming thought that perhaps his friends were playing a joke <u>on</u> him.

1.5. Expressing *any*, *every*, *all*, *never*, and *no (noun)*

1. 一吃东西，什么都忘了。

2. Zhang Daming looked toward the house. He didn't see anyone.

3. Zhang Daming ate the food. Everything was delicious.

1.6 怎么 Verb$_1$, 都/也 Verb$_2$ zěnme Verb$_1$, dōu/yě Verb$_2$
no matter how (one) does Verb$_1$, Verb$_2$

1. There was too much food. No matter how he ate, he couldn't finish it.

2. Where is the painting? No matter how I look for it I can't find it!

1.7. 把 bǎ

1. 不但有时候忘了做饭，也有时候把吃饭都忘了。

2. 他把大夫请来，回家的时候，在路上看见家里房子上头有很多烟。

3. 后来他把吃的拿出来放在桌子上，坐下就吃。

4. 张大明把所有的东西都吃完了。

5. Zhang Daming took the snacks and ate them up.

6. Zhang Daming took the picture and brought it home.

7. Old Mr. Gao took the painting and presented it to Zhang Daming.

1.8. Manner adverbials

1. 他们都说他画得真好。

2. Meizhen sewed the clothing quickly.

3. Old Mr. Gao painted the painting well.

4. Old Mr. Gao painted the picture extremely quickly.

1.9. Verb 了 le Verb *did an action briefly or quickly*

1. Zhang Daming quickly thanked Old Mr. Gao.

2. Zhang Daming's friends took a look at the painting.

1.10. 一 yī VP_1 (就 jiù) VP_2 *as soon as VP_1, VP_2*

1. 再一看，火上有做好了的吃的东西。

2. 一吃东西什么都忘了 。

3. As soon as Zhang Daming saw the painting he spoke to it.

4. When Zhang Daming looked, the beautiful woman wasn't on the painting anymore.

1.11. Describing a noun with a description: description + 的 de + Noun

1. 那个时候，正好七八月，是最忙的时候。

2. The food that was on the fire was very delicious.

3. The painting that Old Mr. Gao painted has no mountains or water.

4. The beautiful woman in the painting is not able to cook.

1.12. The verb suffix 着 zhe

1. 他怕是昨天晚上做点心的时候，火还着着，也许房子里着火了。

2. 你看着，我放在这儿了。

3. Zhang Daming, holding a piece of white paper, went to see Mr. Gao.

4. Zhang Daming's friends, eating snacks, spoke with Meizhen.

1.13. The verb suffix 过 guo

1. I have never seen that beautiful woman before.

2. Have you eaten Chinese food before?

3. Zhang Daming has never painted a picture before.

1.14. 怎么回事 zěnme huí shì *What's going on?*

1. 他想来想去，不知道是怎么回事。

2. As soon as Zhang Daming saw the food on the table he thought, "What's going on?"

3. Zhang Daming asked old Mr. Gao, "What's going on?"

1.15. 帮忙 bāng máng *help*

1. 老张，你能不能帮我一点儿忙？

2. 张大明最愿意帮朋友忙，所以他听见这个话就立刻到城里头去了。

3. Old Mr. Gao wanted to help Zhang Daming.

4. The lady in the painting was willing to help.

Chapter 1 Reading Comprehension Questions

Answer the following questions in complete Chinese sentences based on the story.

1. 张大明每天跟朋友做什么？

2. 张大明的朋友，谁没进去高老先生的家？

3. 张大明有了画儿以后，家里的事情不愿意做了。为什么？

4. 张大明有一天回家的时候看见了什么奇怪的事情 ？（ 着火 ）

5. 张大明想是谁给他做饭的 ？

6. 他后来想一定不是他朋友跟他开玩笑的。为什么？

第二章：画儿上的美人

张大明那天做工的时候，也忘不了昨天那件奇怪的事。老是想那个饭是谁做的。当然要是真是画儿上的人下来了，那是太好了。可是怎么能有那样儿的事呢？

他的朋友们看他做工的时候老想事情，就有人问他说，「你想什么呢？是不是有女朋友了？」

他因为那件事情太奇怪。不愿意告诉人。所以他跟他朋友说，「别开玩笑了，我怎么能有女朋友？我昨天夜里睡觉没睡好。」

他朋友说，「那么你早一点儿回去吧。」他正想早一点儿回去看看，所以他说，也好。

那天他比平常早回去两个多钟头。他到了家，没进去。慢慢儿地走到窗户那儿，往里看。你知道他看见什么了吗？

张大明从窗户往屋子里一看，真有一个女的坐在那儿缝衣裳呢。他看不见那个女人的脸，可是衣裳是画儿上的那个人的衣裳，头发是画儿上那个人的头发。再看看那张画儿，画儿上没有人了。就有一张白纸。

张大明看了以后，站在窗户外头，不知道怎么办好。

差不多有一两分钟的工夫，他什么都不能想。他不信能真有这样儿的事。所以他看了又看，想了又想，最后他得想现在应当怎么办。

他想跑进去，跟她说话，可是说什么呢？又怕那个女人一听见他进去，就立刻回到画儿上去，不下来了。怎么办好呢？

他想来想去，怎么想也想不出好法子来。你说他应当怎么办呢？

张大明在窗户外头想了半天，一点儿法子都没有。最后他慢慢儿地把门开开，进去以后先走到那张画儿那儿去。——那个时候已经是一张白纸了。不是画儿了。

他为什么要先到画儿那儿去呢？因为他怕那个女人看见他，又跑到画上去。

他站在画儿底下，心里有一点儿着急。又有一点儿不好意思。那个女的还是缝衣裳。他不知道那个女的听见没听见他进来了。所以他在那儿站了有半分钟，什么也没说，什么也没想。心里跟一张白纸一样。

后来他往前走了一点儿。那个女的还是缝衣裳，没看他。他慢慢儿地走过去，用手一拿那件衣裳，那个女的就站起来了。他不知不觉地说，「谢谢你，我真得谢谢你。」

张大明跟那个女的说，「我真得谢谢你。」说着脸就红了。很不好意思。那个女的没觉得不好意思。看着张大明笑了笑说，「不谢，不谢。」张大明还是不知道说什么好。想了半天，才说，「你什么时候下来的。」那个女的说，「我早上就下来了。下来以后先睡了一会儿觉。因为在画儿上的时候不能睡觉。起来以后就做饭，把饭做好了，就缝衣裳。还没缝完呢，你就回来了。你今天为什么这么早就回来了？」张大明说，「因为我想知道是不是真是你下来给我做饭，给我缝衣裳。我真不知道怎么谢谢你才好。」那个女的说，「这没什么，我也很愿意帮你的忙。」张大明说，「你不要回到画儿上去了，就在这儿吧。」他说着就把那张白纸拿下来，放在箱子里了。

张大明问那个女的说，「你姓什么，名字叫什么？」她说，「我没有姓，也没有名字。」张大明说，「一个人怎么能没有姓没有名字呢？」她说：「因为那张画儿上没写着我的姓跟名字，也没有人叫过我，我怎么知道我叫什么呢？」张大明说：「你看，我姓张，你也姓张好不好？你又会做饭，又能做衣裳，还对我这么好。你不要走了。就在这儿跟我一块儿住吧。我家里也没有别人，我想你也没有家。以后这儿就是你的家。这个家就是我们的，你愿意吗？」那个女的心里很愿意，可是没说什么。就看着张大明笑了笑。他们两个人跪在地下，拜天拜地，就结婚了。

结婚以后，第二天，他们请了好些朋友到他们家里来看看。

那位高老先生也来了。因为那张画儿，是高老先生画的，所以人人都想请他画一张美人。可是高老先生说：「我告诉你们吧。我给我自己画了很多张美人，到现在还一个都没下来呢。」

张大明问高老先生说：「我的太太当然应当姓张，可是她叫什么名字呢？」

高老先生想了想，说：「这个画的美人，现在已经是一个真的美人了。我们就叫她美真，好不好？」他们都说，很好。

张大明还是每天早上出去做工。美真在家里做饭，做衣裳。过了些日子以后，他们吃的穿的都比以前好一点儿了。

Chapter 2 Vocabulary

老(是)	lǎo (shì)	*ADV*	*always*
那样(儿)	nàyàng (nàyàr)	*SP + M*	*that kind (of)*
告诉	gàosu	*V*	*inform, tell*
正	zhèng	*ADV*	*right at that moment*
窗户	chuānghu	*N*	*window*
脸	liǎn	*N*	*face*
头发	tóufa	*N*	*hair*
怎么办好	zěnme bàn hǎo	*VP*	*what best to do*
信	xìn	*V*	*believe*
法子	fǎzi	*N*	*plan, solution*
纸	zhǐ	*N*	*paper*
底下	dǐxià	*N + LOC*	*beneath*
着急	zháojí	*AV*	*anxious, excited*
不好意思	bù hǎo yìsi	*AVP*	*embarrassed*
听见	tīngjiàn	*RV*	*hear*
不知不觉地	bù zhī bù juéde	*ADV P*	*involuntarily*
红	hóng	*AV*	*red*
箱子	xiāngzi	*N*	*box, trunk*
住	zhù	*V*	*live (in a place), reside*
跪	guì	*V*	*kneel*
拜	bài	*V*	*bow*
拜天拜地	bài tiān bài dì	*VO, V O*	*bow to heaven and earth*

结婚	jiéhūn	*V*	*marry*
好些	hǎoxiē	*AVP*	*a good many*
穿	chuān	*V*	*wear*

Chapter 2 Structure Notes

2.1 Comparisons with 比 bǐ *more than*

比 bǐ is used to compare two things (nouns or noun phrases) and to indicate that the first thing has *more of* some property than the second thing. The property is expressed an Adjectival Verb (AV) or an Adjectival Verb Phrase (AVP):

> NP_1 比 bǐ NP_2 AV(P)
> NP_1 *is more* AV(P) than NP_2

> 我比他高。
> Wǒ bǐ tā gāo.
> *I am taller than he is.*

> 这本书比那本书有意思。
> Zhè běn shū bǐ nà běn shū yǒu yìsī.
> *This book is more interesting than that book.*

In this example from Chapter 2, the things that are being compared are presented in [square brackets].

> 过了些日子以后，[他们吃的穿的] 都<u>比</u> [以前] <u>好一点儿</u>了。
> Guò le xiē rìzi yǐhòu, [tāmen chī de chuān de] dōu <u>bǐ</u> [yǐqián] <u>hǎo yīdiǎr</u> le.
> *After a few days, [what they ate and what they wore] was <u>a little better than</u> [before].*

2.2. Resultative Verbs

2.2.1 Basic Resultative Verbs

Verbs such as 吃 chī *eat*, 学 xué *study*, 说 shuō *speak, say*, 听 tīng *listen*, and 买 mǎi *shop* refer to open-ended activities. In order to indicate the conclusion or result of these activities, follow the activity verb with a *resultative ending*. The activity with the resultative ending is a *resultative verb*.

Here are some common resultative endings and the meanings they contribute to an activity:

> 懂 dǒng *understand*
>
> 完 wán *finish/complete*
>
> 好 hǎo *reach a successful conclusion*
>
> 错 cuò *do wrong or mistakenly*

见 jiàn *perceive* (only used with perception verbs like 看 kàn and 听 tīng)

着 zháo *accomplish*

As the following examples illustrate, a single activity verb can take different resultative endings. Each ending indicates a different result or conclusion for the activity.

Activity Verb	**Activity Verb + RV ending**
看 kàn *look, read*	看见 kànjiàn *look to the point of seeing: see*
	看懂 kàndǒng *read to the point of understanding: understand by reading*
	看完 kànwán *read to the point of finishing: finish reading*
做 zuò *do, make*	做完 zuòwán *do to the point of finishing: finish*
	做好 zuòhǎo *do to a successful conclusion*
	做错 zuòcuò *do incorrectly*
说 shuō *speak, say*	说完 shuōwán *finish speaking*
	说好 shuōhǎo *reach an agreement (by conversing)*
	说错 shuōcuò *say incorrectly*
听 tīng *listen*	听见 tīngjian *hear*
	听懂 tīngdǒng *understand (by listening)*
	听错 tīngcuò *hear incorrectly*
	听完 tīngwán *finish listening*
买 mǎi *buy*	买错 mǎicuò *buy incorrectly (buy the wrong item)*
	买着 mǎizháo *succeed in buying*

Here are some sentences from Chapter 2 that include resultative verbs. The resultative verbs are underlined in each example.

起来以后就做饭，把饭<u>做好</u>了，就缝衣裳。
Qǐlai yǐhòu jiù zuò fàn, bǎ fàn <u>zuòhǎo</u> le, jiù féng yīshang.
After (I) got up (I) cooked, and when (I) <u>finished cooking</u> (the meal) (I) mended the clothes.

他不知道那个女的<u>听见</u>没<u>听见</u>他进来。
Tā bù zhīdao nàge nǚ de <u>tīngjian</u> méi <u>tīngjian</u> tā jìnlái.
He didn't know if that woman had <u>heard</u> him come in or not.

2.2.2 The Potential Form of Resultative Verbs with 得 de and 不 bu

To indicate that *it is possible* or *it is not possible to reach a conclusion*, add 得 de or 不 bu between the activity verb and the resultative ending. Notice that in this structure, 得 de and 不 bu occur in neutral tone.

得 de indicates possibility. That is, it indicates that it is possible to reach the result or conclusion indicated by the ending.

看得懂 kàndedǒng *it is possible to read to the point of understanding; one can read and understand*

做得完 zuòdewán *it is possible to do to the point of finishing; one can finish doing the action*

不 bu indicates impossibility. That is, it indicates that it is impossible to reach the result or conclusion indicated by the ending.

看不懂 kànbudǒng *one can read but cannot understand*

做不完 zuòbuwán *one can do but cannot finish*

The following sentences from the story include a resultative verb in the *potential* form. The resultative verb is underlined.

(张大明)怎么睡也<u>睡不着</u>。*(Chapter 1)*
(Zhāng Dàmíng) zěnme shuì yě shuìbuzháo.
Now matter how (Zhang Daming) tried to sleep, he <u>couldn't sleep</u>.

他<u>看不见</u>那个女人的脸，可是衣裳是画儿上的那个人的衣裳，头发是画儿上那个人的头发。*(Chapter 2)*

Tā <u>kànbujiàn</u> nàge nǚren de liǎn, kěshì yīshang shì huàr shàng de nàge rén de yīshang, tóufa shì huàrshàng nàge rén de tóufa.

He <u>couldn't see</u> the woman's face, but her clothing was the clothing of the lady in the painting, her hair was the hair of the lady in the painting.

2.2.3 The Potential endings 得 deliǎo and 不了 buliǎo

The potential endings 得了 deliǎo and 不了 buliǎo can follow any verb that refers to an action. These endings indicate that the action of the verb itself can (得了 deliǎo) or cannot (不了 buliǎo) be done.

Verb - 得了 deliǎo	Verb - 不了 buliǎo
做得了 zuòdeliǎo *can do, able to do*	做不了 zuòbuliǎo *cannot do, unable to do*
吃得了 chīdeliǎo *can eat, able to eat*	吃不了 chībuliǎo *cannot eat, unable to eat*

The following sentence from Chapter 2 includes a potential ending.

> 张大明那天做工的时候，也忘不了昨天那件奇怪的事。
> Zhāng Dàmíng nà tiān zuò gōng de shíhou, yě wàngbuliǎo zuótiān nà jiàn qíguài de shì.
> *That day when Zhang Daming was working, he couldn't forget yesterday's strange incident.*

Note the difference between the resultative endings in Note 2.2.2 and the potential endings presented here. Resultative endings refer to the way in which the action of the verb concludes. Potential endings indicate whether the action of the verb itself can or cannot be done.

2.3. 不知道 Verb 什么好 bù zhīdao Verb shénme hǎo
don't know what best to Verb

Any verb that refers to an action can be used in this pattern. In this example from the story, the verb is underlined.

> 张大明还是不知道说什么好。
> Zhāng Dàmíng háishi bù zhīdao shuō shénme hǎo.
> *Zhang Daming didn't know what best to say.*

2.4. Verb 了 le 又 yòu Verb *did an action repeatedly in the past*

> 所以他看了又看，想了又想，最后他得想现在应当怎么办。
> Suóyǐ tā kàn le yòu kàn, xiǎng le yòu xiǎng, zuìhòu tā děi xiǎng xiànzài yīngdāng zěnmebàn.
> *So he looked and looked, and he thought and thought. Finally, he had to figure out what to do now.*

2.5. 一点(儿) NP 都/也 NEG + Verb
yīdiǎn (yīdiǎr) NP dōu/yě NEG + Verb
not even Verb a little of the NP

> 张大明在窗户外头想了半天，一点儿法子都没有。
> Zhāng Dàmíng zài chuānghu wàitou xiǎng le bàntiān, yīdiǎr fǎzi dōu méi yǒu.
> *Zhang Daming thought for a long time outside of the window, he didn't have any plan at all.*

In this pattern, the object of the verb occurs before the negated verb, instead of in the neutral position for the object, after the verb. 一点儿 yīdiǎr is the colloquial Beijing pronunciation of 一点 yīdiǎn.

> 他一点儿饭也没吃。
> Tā yīdiǎr fàn yě méi chī.
> *He didn't even eat a little food.* [吃飯 chī fàn *eat (food)*]
> 他一点儿钱都没有。
> Tā yīdiǎn qián dōu méi yǒu.
> *He doesn't have any money.*
> *(He doesn't even have a little money.)* [有錢 yǒu qián *have money*]

2.6. 才 cái *(and) only then*

才 cái indicates a relationship of sequence between two events. It indicates that the second event occurs *only after* the first one. 才 cái can often be translated with the expression *only then* or *and only then*.

> VP_1 才 cái VP_2
> *VP_1 occurs and only then does VP_2 occur*

才 cái must occur immediately before the second VP in the sequence.

> 他想了半天，才说，「你什么时候下来的？」
> Tā xiǎng le bàntiān, cái shuō, "Nǐ shénme shíhou xiàlai de?"
> *He thought for a long time and only then said, "When did you come down?"*

Even if the sentence describes a completed event, if 才 cái occurs in the sentence, 了 le does not occur to mark completion.

> 她昨天晚上做完了事才回家。
> Tā zuótiān wǎnshang zuòwán le shì cái huí jiā.
> *Last night she finished her work and only then returned home.*

Chapter 2 Structure Exercises

Using the Chapter 2 *Structure Notes* as your guide, translate the Chinese sentences to English and the English sentences to Chinese. The Chinese sentences have been selected from Chapter 2.

2.1 Comparisons with 比 bǐ *more than*

1. 那天他比平常早回去两个钟头。

2. Zhang Daming is more anxious than other people.

3. Meizhen was more embarrassed than Zhang Daming.

2.2. Resultative Verbs

1. 还没缝完呢，你就回来了。

2. 她做事做得很快，别人一天才能做完的事，她一两个钟头就做好了。

3. 别人做不了的事，不知道为什么，她一做，不大的工夫就都做完了。

Translate the underlined expressions with resultative verbs:

4. Last night, Zhang Daming could not fall asleep.

5. Meizhen heard Zhang Daming come in.

6. Zhang Daming asked Old Mr. Gao if he finished painting the picture.

7. Zhang Daming wrote Meizhen's name wrong. (use 把 bǎ)

8. Zhang Daming's friends are unable to cook food.

9. The lady in the painting is certainly unable to talk!

2.3. 不知道 Verb 什么好 bù zhīdao Verb shénme hǎo
don't know what best to Verb

1. Zhang Daming's friends didn't know what best to sing.

2. Meizhen didn't know what best to do.

3. Old Mr. Gao didn't know what best to paint.

4. We didn't know what best to wear.

2.4. V 了 le 又 yòu V *did an action repeatedly in the past*

1. Zhang Daming listened and listened. Was there a person outside of the house?

2. Zhang Daming called and called but the lady in the painting did not come down.

2.5. 一点(儿) NP 都/也 NEG + Verb
yīdiǎn (yīdiǎr) NP dōu/yě + Negation + Verb
not even Verb a little of the NP

1. Zhang Daming didn't say anything. (说话 shuō huà)

2. Mr. Gao doesn't want any money. (要钱 yào qián)

3. The lady in the painting did not eat any food. (吃饭 chī fàn)

2.7. 才 cái *only then*

1. Old Mr. Gao painted for two days and only then finished painting.

2. Zhang Daming looked and looked at the painting and only then went to sleep.

Chapter 2 Reading Comprehension Questions

Answer the following questions in complete Chinese sentences based on the story. Use the parenthesized grammatical pattern or vocabulary item where provided.

1. 张大明为什么早一点回家了？

2. 张大明为什么没跑进屋子去？（怕）

3. 张大明一 进了屋子为什么就站在白纸底下？（回）

4. 美人从画儿上下来以后先做了什么？为什么 ？

5. 张大明跟美真是在哪儿结婚的？

第三章：逮鸽子

美真很有本事，不但会做衣裳会做饭，差不多什么都会做。也很愿意帮别人的忙。谁有什么难办的事情都来找她。她老是高高兴兴地给人做好了。所以人都很喜欢她。

她做事做得很快，别人一天才能做完的事，她一两个钟头就做好了。别人做不了的事，不知道为什么，她一做，不大的工夫就都做完了。

有一天美真正在家里做衣裳，她听见外头有人哭。她开开门看看，问他们怎么了。外头那两个人说，「因为国王每天要吃两个鸽子，所以叫我们两个人一天逮两个鸽子给国王送去。可是今天我们用了一天的工夫，一个鸽子都没逮着，我们怕国王生气，不知道怎么办好。所以就哭了。」

那两个人还说，给那国王做事很不容易。国王很爱生气，一生气就打人。还有时候一生气就把人杀了。谁也没有法子。

美真没听说过国王的事情，她很想多知道一点儿。所以她问，「给国王做事这么难，那么为什么你们还给他做事呢？」

一个人说，「不给他逮鸽子，我们吃什么呢？要是不给国王做事，得上税。上税的钱比买两个鸽子的钱多得多。要是不给他做事，我们一天逮十个鸽子，也不够吃的。」

美真一想，他说得很对。她跟大明两个人不是也得上很多钱的税吗？要是不是他们做事做得快，也许每天都不够吃的。

美真跟那两个人说了一会儿话。那两个人说，「不早了，我们去逮鸽子去吧。老在这儿说话办不了事。再见吧。」

美真说，「别走，请进来喝点儿茶。我还想再听听这个国王的事情。」

一个人说，「谢谢你，今天我们不进去了。我们还有事呢，等以后有工夫的时候再说吧。」美真说，「忙什么？坐坐再走。」那两个人，有一个人有一点儿着急，他说，「你没事，当然不用忙，天快黑了，要是今天我们没有鸽子，怎么回去见国王？别说了，快走吧。」

美真看他一定要走，就笑着说，「别着急，别着急。不是就是两个鸽子的事情么？等一会儿，我给你们两个。」那两个人一听都高兴了。美真就问这个问那个。问了很多话。那两个人想美真一会儿就给他们两个鸽子，他们不必去逮了，也就不必忙了，所以也就不着急了。后来天已经很晚了，他们要走了，有一个人说，「请你给我们鸽子吧。」美真说，你们等一会儿。她说着就进去拿了一张白纸，用纸做了两个纸鸽子。那两个人在外头看着不懂是怎么回事。

那两个人在门外头看见美真用纸做了两个纸鸽子，先不明白美真是什么意思，后来一想也许是跟他们开玩笑。有一个人就真生气了。在门外头说，「再见吧。我们走了。我们没有工夫跟你开玩笑。」

美真说，「别走，别走。等一等，给你们这两个鸽子。」

有一个人说，「要不然我们就等一等看看是怎么回事。」他们两个人就站在门外头看着，看美真做什么。

美真走到门那儿，对着两个纸鸽子吹了一口气，两个鸽子就飞起来了。

那两个人看见纸鸽子飞起来了，觉得奇怪极了。立刻就把两个鸽子都逮着了。他们不懂是怎么回事。他们有了鸽子，也就什么都不问了。

那两个人有了鸽子了，就不着急了。又跟美真说了半天话，才拿着鸽子高高兴兴地走了。

那两个人在路上走着的时候，有一个人说，要是这两个鸽子在国王吃的时候，又变成纸的，那怎么办呢？

那个人一想也对。可是有什么法子呢？他说，要是我们送到了的时候是真鸽子，那就行了。他吃的时候，是不是纸的，那就不是我们的事了。

他们两个人把鸽子送到了，就回家吃饭去了。他们吃完饭，过了一会儿，忽然外头有人叫门，说国王叫他们要问他们的话。这两个人一听，说，坏了。一定是鸽子变成纸的了。可是没法子，不愿意去，也不能不去。

他们见着国王，国王说今天的鸽子特别好吃，问他们是在什么地方逮的。

那两个人听说那两个鸽子特别好吃，他们就放了心了。他们知道不是那两个鸽子又变成纸的了。可是他们也不愿意说那两个鸽子是纸做的。他们听见国王问，他们就说那天一直到很晚他们还没逮着鸽子，所以就去买了两个鸽子送来了。国王问他们是在什么地方买的，他们就说是一个很好看的太太卖给他们的。他们就把美真住的地方告诉国王了。

他们两个人走了以后，国王把他手下的一个大官叫来，告诉他张大明住的地方，叫他第二天到张大明家去，叫他们一天送两个鸽子来。

第二天那个大官带着两个人到张大明家去了。见着张大明，跟张大明说国王叫他每天送两个鸽子去。一定要在吃晚饭以前送到。

张大明听了，不懂是怎么回事。因为昨天美真做的事，他一点都不知道。他正要问是怎么回事，那个大官已经走了。

美真告诉大明说，「你知道我们现在上税上得很多。我的意思是想法子少上一点儿税。」

她的话当然大明不懂。因为美真昨天做的事他一点儿都不知道。

大明问，「这是怎么回事？为什么国王叫人到我们这儿来要鸽子？我们怎么能有鸽子？一天给他送两个鸽子去，谁送去？」

美真说，「你别着急，听我慢慢儿告诉你。」美真这才把昨天逮鸽子人哭，她给他们做了两个纸鸽子的事情跟大明说了。美真还说，「听那两个人说，他们给国王做事，可以不上税。我们现在每天给国王两个鸽子，不是也可以不上税吗？」

Chapter 3 Vocabulary

本事	běnshi	*N*	*talent, ability*
高高兴兴地	gāogāo xìngxìng de	*ADV P*	*happily*
哭	kū	*V*	*cry*
怎么了？	zěnme le?	*Question*	*what's the matter?*
国王	guówáng	*N*	*king*
鸽子	gēzi	*N*	*pigeon*
逮	dǎi	*V*	*catch*
生气	shēng qì	*VP (VO)*	*be angry, become angry*
杀	shā	*V*	*kill*
税	shuì	*N*	*taxes*
上税	shàng shuì	*VP (VO)*	*pay taxes*
喝	hē	*V*	*drink*
茶	chá	*N*	*tea*
等	děng	*V*	*wait (wait until)*
不用	bú yòng	*MVP*	*do not have to*
不必	bú bì	*MVP*	*do not have to*
懂	dǒng	*V*	*understand*
吹	chuī	*V*	*blow*
一口气	yī kǒu qì	*NP*	*one mouthful of air*
变成	biànchéng	*V*	*change into*
行	xíng	*V*	*okay*
忽然	hūrán	*ADV*	*suddenly*

特别	tèbié	*INT*	*especially*
地方	dìfang	*N*	*place*
手下	shǒuxià	*N*	*subordinate*
大官	dà guān	*N*	*government official*
带	dài	*V*	*take along*
慢慢(儿)地	mànmān de (mànmār de)	*ADV P*	*slowly*

Chapter 3 Structure Notes

3.1. Describing how an action is performed

To describe how an action is performed, precede the action with the description + 地 de. Here is an example of this structure from Chapter 3.

> 那两个人，。。。拿着鸽子，高高兴兴地走了。
> Nà liǎng gè rén, . . . ná zhe gēzi, gāogāo xìngxìng de zǒu le.
> *Those two people, . . . holding the pigeons, went happily away.*

地 de is sometimes omitted.

> 听我慢慢儿告诉你。
> Tīng wǒ mànmār gàosu nǐ.
> *Listen while I slowly tell you about it.*

3.2. Linking events with connecting words

Connecting words link two events and indicate a relationship between them. Here is a summary of the connecting words used in 画儿上的美人 with examples from the story that show how they are used.

3.2.1. Contrast

可是 kěshì *but*

> Sentence$_1$, 可是 Sentence$_2$
> *Sentence$_1$, but Sentence$_2$*

> 别人家里有太太，有孩子，可是张大明回到家里，什么人都没有。
> Bié ren jiālǐ yǒu tàitai, yǒu háizi, kěshì Zhāng Dàmíng huí dào jiā lǐ, shénme rén dōu méi yǒu.
> *In other people's families there are a wife and children, but when Zhang Daming returns home, there is no one there. (Chapter 1)*

3.2.2. Alternatives

要不然 yàobùrán *otherwise*

> Sentence$_1$. 要不然 Sentence$_2$
> *S$_1$. Otherwise S$_2$*

> 三天里头一定得给我做好。要不然我就把你杀了。
> Sān tiān lǐtou yīdìng děi gěi wǒ zuòhǎo. Yàobùrán wǒ jiù bǎ nǐ shā le.
> *You definitely must finish it for me within three days. Otherwise I will kill you. (Chapter 6)*

有一个人说「<u>要不然</u>我们就等一等看看是怎么回事。」
Yǒu yīge rén shuō "<u>yàobùrán</u> wǒmen jiù děng yī děng kàn kàn shì zěnme huí shì." *One person said "<u>otherwise</u> we can just wait for a while and see what's going on." (Chapter 3)*

3.2.3. Additional Information

不但 búdàn *not only*

美真很有本事，<u>不但</u>会做衣裳会做饭，差不多什么都会做。
Měizhēn hěn yǒu běnshi, <u>búdàn</u> huì zuò yīshang huì zuò fàn, chàbuduō shénme dōu huì zuò.
Meizhen is really talented. She can <u>not only</u> make clothing and cook, she can do almost everything. (Chapter 3)

不但 búdàn is often paired with 也 yě *also*:

不但 Verb Phrase$_1$ 也 Verb Phrase$_2$
not only Verb Phrase$_1$ but also Verb Phrase$_2$

高老先生不但会画山水，也会画人。
Gāo lǎo xiānsheng búdàn huì huà shānshuǐ, yě huì huà rén.
Old Mr. Gao can not only paint landscapes, he can also paint people.

Although it does not occur in this story, 不但 búdàn is often paired with the connecting word 而且 érqiě *also, in addition.*

不但 Verb Phrase$_1$, 而且 Verb Phrase$_2$
not only Verb Phrase$_1$, (also) Verb Phrase$_2$

美真不但很好看，而且很有本事。
Měizhēn búdàn hěn hǎo kàn, érqiě hěn yǒu běnshi.
Meizhen is not only very pretty, she is also very talented.

3.2.4. Cause and Effect or Reason and Result

因为 yīnwei *because*...所以 suóyǐ *therefore*

因为 yīnwei *because* and 所以 suóyǐ *therefore* may occur together in the same sentence, or they may each occur alone. When they occur together, if their clauses have different subjects, each connecting word occurs before the subject of its clause.

因为 Clause$_1$, 所以 Clause$_2$
Because Clause$_1$, (therefore) Clause$_2$

因为美真很有本事，所以张大明很喜欢他。
Yīnwei Měizhēn hěn yǒu běnshi, suóyǐ Zhāng Dàmíng hěn xǐhuan tā.
Because Meizhen is very talented, (therefore) Zhang Daming likes her a lot.

因为 yīnweì and 所以 suóyǐ may also occur directly before the verb phrase.

我们怕国王生气，不知道怎麼办好。所以就哭了。
Wǒmen pà guówáng shēngqì, bù zhīdào zěnme bàn hǎo. Suóyǐ jiù kū le.
We were afraid that the king would get angry, and we didn't know what best to do. So we cried. (Chapter 3)

因为国王每天要吃两个鸽子，所以叫我们两个人一天逮两个鸽子给国王送去。
Yīnwéi guówáng měitiān yào chī liǎng gè gēzi，suóyǐ jiào wǒmen liǎng gè rén yī tiān dǎi liǎng gè gēzi gěi guówáng sòng qù.
Because the king wants to eat two pigeons every day, (they) told the two of us to catch two pigeons every day to present to the king. (Chapter 3)

他们因为没有钱，所以得给国王逮鸽子。
Tāmen yīnweì méi yǒu qián, suóyǐ děi gěi guówáng dǎi gēzi.
Because they do not have any money, they have to catch pigeons for the king.

3.2.5. "if . . . then" conditions

要是 yàoshi *if*

要是 Sentence_1, Sentence_2

要是不给国王做事，得上税。
Yàoshì bù gěi guówáng zuò shì, děi shàng shuì.
If (we) do not work for the king, (we) have to pay taxes. (Chapter 3)

When 要是 yàoshi is used, 就 jiù often occurs in Sentence_2. 就 jiù occurs right before the verb phrase.

要是我们送到了的时候是真鸽子，那就行了。
Yàoshi wǒmen sòng dào le de shíhou shì zhēn gēzi, nà jiù xíng le.
If they are real pigeons when we deliver them, then it is okay. (Chapter 3)

Chapter 3 Structure Exercises

3.1. Describing how an action is performed

Translate these Chinese sentences from the story into English, and translate the English sentences into Chinese, describing the action with description ＋地 de.

1. 张大明慢慢儿地走到窗户那儿。

2. 他不知不觉地说「谢谢你。」

3. Old Mr. Gao slowly walked home.

4. The king happily ate the pigeons.

3.2. Linking events with connecting words

Complete these sentences in Chinese based on the facts of the story.

1. 张大明家里没有人，所以

2. 高老先生给张大明画了一张画儿，可是

3. 美真很会做事。她不但

4. 因为逮鸽子的人

5. 美真想她一定要帮那两个人的忙。要不然

Chapter 3 Reading Comprehension Questions

Answer the following questions in complete Chinese sentences based on the story.

1. 有一天美真听见外头有人哭。那两个人为什么哭？

2. 逮鸽子的人为什么给国王做事？

3. 有一个人很着急不要进去喝茶。他为什很着急 ？

4. 逮鸽子的人怕给国王送那两个鸽 子。为什么？

第四章：送鸽子

第二天早上，美真又用纸做了两个纸鸽子，叫大明送去。大明说，「这纸鸽子怎么能变成真鸽子呢？」美真说，「你听我的话，一定错不了。我叫你做什么，你就做什么好了。」大明还是不太信，可是他没说什么。把两个纸鸽子放在口袋儿里，看了看美真，想了想，就要走。美真把他叫回来，跟他说，「你放心吧，你不用怕。所有的事情，我都想好了，你快去快回来吧。」张大明听了这几句话，就走了。

张大明在路上想，他想纸鸽子怎么能吃呢？他又想要是他把纸鸽子给国王，国王一生气，他怎么办呢？他想到这儿，心里有一点儿怕。又一想他太太说的，「你听我的话，一定错不了。」他也觉得他太太的话错不了。他就又不怕了。

张大明见着国王，他说他是来送鸽子的。国王问他鸽子在什么地方呢？因为他看张大明手里没拿着什么，他想也许张大明把鸽子放在外头了。没想到，张大明把手放在口袋儿里，从口袋里把两个纸鸽子拿出来给国王看。在那儿看的人都觉得很奇怪。国王一看鸽子是纸的，正要说话还没说呢，两个鸽子就都飞起来了。国王那儿的人看见鸽子飞了，都不知道怎么办好。他们就来回跑，要逮那两个鸽子。

国王看见那些人来回地跑，两个鸽子上下地飞。那些人逮了半天也没逮着，后来鸽子飞出去了。

国王看着鸽子飞出去了，谁也没逮着，立刻就很生气。跟他们说，「谁叫这个人到这儿来的？你们看看，这么多人在我前头来回跑，这是怎么回事？告诉他，明天送鸽子的时候，不要他来，叫他太太自己来，我要看看这个女人是一个什么样儿的人。叫他快一点儿出去。」

那些人看见国王生气了，都有一点儿怕，就很快地叫张大明出去了。

张大明到了家，把鸽子飞了，国王生气了的事情跟美真说了，也告诉美真说，国王叫她自己去送鸽子去，要见见她。美真听了说，「别着急，我明天去。我有法子。」

第二天美真自己去了。

国王看见美真这么好看，什么都忘了。他笑了一笑，也不知道说什么好。

他第一句话就说，「你怎么这么好看呢！」他也忘了问她鸽子的事情。

美真站在那儿没说什么，她想听听那个国王还说什么。

国王说，「你是张大明的太太吗？」

美真说，「对了。」

国王又说，「这么好看的一个人，怎么跟一个乡下人结婚呢？我看你不要回去了。就做我的妃子吧。你在我这儿，想吃什么有什么，想穿什么有什么。你想要什么我给你什么。我什么都有，什么都比你们家好。你不要回去了。」

美真一听，很生气。她一点儿也不怕。走到国王的前头，站在那个地方没说话。国王也不知道她要做什么。那些大官看见美真生气了，也看见她走到国王的前头去了。可是没人知道应当怎么办，有的想过去拉住她，又怕国王生气。所以他们就都站在那儿看着。

美真站在那儿，很不客气地说，「你别胡说。」

国王一听，觉得真奇怪。没有人跟他说话说得这样不客气。他不知道应当怎么办。生气也不好，笑也不好。想说话也不知道说什么好。

那个时候，美真又往前走了一点儿，对国王说，「你这个国王，真不是东西。一个国王，应当好好地办国里的事情。应当替平常人想想。可是你这个人，不想办事；不是想吃鸽子，就是要女人。我跟你说，你这样儿的国王，一定做不长。我跟我先生张大明结婚，是我们自己的事情。我们结婚，是因为他爱我，我也喜欢他。有没有东西吃，有没有衣裳穿，那都不要紧。你知道什么？你懂什么？你怎能跟张大明比？张大明什么不比你好？你说话也不想想？真是胡说。」她说着就走出去了。

国王一句话也没有，那些大官也是一句话也没有。他们真是哭也不好，笑也不好，生气也

不好。有一个想过去跟美真说话，要请她回来，可是看美真生气的样子，他知道，说也是没用。所以就叫她走了。

第二天早上，张大明还没出去呢，就听见门外头有人叫门。张大明想谁这么早来呢？他想也许是国王叫人来找他，可是他不知道是什么事。他也想昨天美真跟国王说那样儿不客气的话，国王一定生气了。那么今天来找他一定没什么好事。想到这个地方，心里有点儿怕。可是门外头的人说，「快开门来。」

美真知道张大明有一点儿怕，就说，「不用怕，我跟你一块儿去开门去。」他们两个人就一块儿出去了。

Chapter 4 Vocabulary

错	cuò	*AV*	*mistaken, wrong*
错不了	cuòbuliǎo	*RV*	*unable to be mistaken, can't go wrong*
口袋(儿)	kǒudài (kǒudàr)	*N*	*pocket*
飞起来	fēiqilai	*V + DIR*	*begin to fly*
来回	lái huí	*V + V*	*back and forth*
半天	bàntiān	*N*	*for a long time (literally: a half day)*
乡下	xiāngxià	*N*	*countryside*
乡下人	xiāngxià rén	*NP*	*country bumpkin*
妃子	fēizi	*N*	*imperial concubine*
拉	lā	*V*	*pull*
拉住	lāzhù	*RV*	*restrain, grab hold of*
不客气地	bù kèqi de	*ADV P*	*impolitely*
胡说	hú shuō	*ADV + V*	*talk nonsense*
不是东西	bù shì dōngxi	*VP*	*be nothing, be despicable*
替	tì	*P*	*for, on behalf of*
办事	bàn shì	*VP (VO)*	*do work*
要紧	yàojǐn	*AV*	*important*
叫门	jiào mén	*VP (VO)*	*call at the door*

Chapter 4 Structure Notes

4.1. Expressing *whoever, whatever, whenever*: Question Word 就 jiù Question Word

Mandarin does not have distinct words that are equivalent to *whoever*, *whatever*, or *whenever*. To express these "indefinite" meanings, Mandarin uses content question words in parallel phrases that occur in sequence and have similar or identical structure. 就 jiù occurs at the beginning of the second verb phrase.

> 我叫你做什么你就做什么好了。
> Wǒ jiào nǐ zuò shénme nǐ jiù zuò shénme hǎo le.
> *Do whatever I tell you to do. (Whatever I tell you to do, do it.)*

When used to express indefinite meaning, the question words occur in the same structural position in each of the parallel phrases. For example:

subject

> 谁要去谁就去。
> Shéi yào qù shéi jiù qù.
> *Whoever wants to go should go.*
> *(literally: Whoever wants to go, whoever should go.)*

object

> 你要买什么就买什么。
> Nǐ yào mǎi shénme jiù mǎi shénme.
> *Buy whatever you want.*
> *(literally: You want to buy whatever, then buy whatever.)*

4.2. Person as Location 我这儿 wǒ zhèr

> 国王那儿的人看见鸽子飞了，都不知道怎么办好。
> Guówáng nàr de rén kànjian gēzi fēi le, dōu bù zhīdao zěnme bàn hǎo.
> *The people by the king (at the king's location) saw the pigeons fly, and they all didn't know what best to do.*

In order for a person or a personal pronoun to serve as a location, it must be followed by 这儿 zhèr *here* or 那儿 nàr *there* (or the expressions 这里 zhèli *here* or 那里 nàli *there*). In Mandarin, you do not *go to the king*. You *go to the king's location:* 国王那儿 guówáng nàr. Similarly, you do not *come to me*. You *come to my location*: 我这儿 wǒ zhèr.

4.3. 不是 A 就是 B bù shì A jiù shì B *if it isn't A then it is B*

This structure presents alternatives. Notice that the structure does not include specific words for *if* and *then*. Rather, the meaning is expressed by the structure as a whole. The following sentence from Chapter 4 illustrates this structure.

不是想吃鸽子，就是要女人。
Bù shì xiǎng chī gēzi, jiù shì yào nǚren.
If you are not thinking about eating pigeons, then you are wanting women.

Chapter 4 Structure Exercises

Using the Chapter 4 *Structure Notes* as your guide, translate the Chinese sentences to English and the English sentences to Chinese. The Chinese sentences have been selected from Chapter 4.

4.1. Expressing *whoever, whatever, whenever*: Question Word 就 jiù Question Word

1. 你在我这儿，想吃什么有什么，想穿什么有什么。

2. 你想要什么我給你什么。

3. You must do whatever the King tells you to do. (Whatever the King tells you to do, you must do.)

4. Zhang Daming said to Mr. Gao, "Paint whatever you want." (You want to paint whatever, then paint whatever.)

4.2. Person as Location 我这儿 wǒ zhèr

1. The King said to Meizhen, "Come to me."

2. Zhang Daming said to his friends, "Let's go over to Mr. Gao's to see the painting."

4.3. 不是 A 就是 B bù shì A jiù shì B *if it isn't A then it is B*

1. Meizhen is busy every day. If she isn't cooking dinner, she is making paper pigeons.

2. Old Mr. Gao really likes to paint (pictures). If he isn't painting landscapes, he is painting people.

Chapter 4 Narrative Practice

Write an essay in which you describe the attempts of 张大明 to present pigeons to the king. Use the following structures and vocabulary in your narrative.

送 sòng	(chapter 1)
拿 ná	(chapter 1)
来回飞 lái huí fēi	(chapter 4)
逮着 dǎizháo	(chapter 3 and resultative verbs, chapter 2)
把 bǎ	(chapter 1)
怎么回事 zěnme huí shì	(chapter 1)
一 yī VP_1 就 jiù VP_2	(chapter 1)
因为 yīnweì	(chapter 3)
可是 kěshì	(chapter 3)
不但 búdàn	(chapter 3)
要不然 yàobùrán	(chapter 3)

Chapter 4 Reading Comprehension Questions

Answer the following questions in complete Chinese sentences based on the story.

1. 张大明为什么怕给国王送鸽子？

2. 张大明送了鸽子，看的人都觉得奇怪。为什么？

3. 国王为什么要美真自己来送鸽子？

4. 大官为什么没跟美真说话？

5. 第二天早上有人叫张大明的门。张大明为什么怕开门？

第五章：赛马

他们把门开开一看，那个人就说，「我是国王叫我来的。昨天张太太说张大明什么都比国王好，国王很生气。所以国王明天要跟张大明赛马，跟他比一比，看看谁的马跑得快。要是张大明的马不能跑到国王的前头，张太太就得去做国王的妃子。明天早上骑着你的马，到东门外头去等国王，别晚了。」他说完了就走了。

张大明站在那儿，站了半天，什么都不知道了。自己也不知道想什么，也许什么都没想。过了一会儿，美真叫他进去，他才明白过来。就跟着美真进去了。

张大明听见美真的话就进去了。心里很着急。因为：第一，他不会骑马。第二，他也没有马。他看着他太太说，「这怎么办呢？」

美真说，「不要紧，我有法子。你到铺子去买些白纸来。我可以给你做一个马，我做的马，比什么马跑得都快。」

张大明想她用纸做的鸽子，可以飞，那么用纸做的马也一定可以跑。可是，有了马以后，还是得用人骑，骑马也不是一件容易的事。骑着马，也许那个马可以跑，可是人骑在马上，骑得住骑不住呢？所以他跟美真说，「你做的马也许能跑，也许比什么马跑得都快。可是我不会骑，也是没用。」

美真说，「我做的马不会骑的人也能骑。骑在我的马上，就跟坐在地下一样。你不用怕，快去买纸去吧。」

张大明把纸买来以后，他们用了一夜的工夫，把马做好了。那个马跟真的差不多，可是还是纸马。美真对着马吹了一口气，那个马就活了。美真说，「你骑上。」大明骑上马，马立刻就跑了。

美真知道张大明一定跑在国王的前头，所以她也没去看。

张大明骑在马上，心里有一点儿怕，可是跑了一会儿，他觉得骑在马上跟坐在地上一样，所以他就不怕了。

他到了东门外头，国王也来了。国王骑着一个黑马。当然那是最好最快的马。

国王看见张大明，就跟他说，「昨天我叫人到你家去，我想他把话已经跟你说明白了。」

张大明没说什么。

国王又说，「好了，没什么说的，你跟我从这儿跑到前头那条河边儿上，再回来。看看你的马快，还是我的马快。我说一，二，三，我们就跑。」他说完了，就说，「一，二，三。」他把「一」字说得又长又慢，可是「二」跟「三」两个字说得很快。张大明没想到。所以国王的马已经跑出去了，张大明才知道他应当跑了。所以他们刚一跑的时候，国王的黑马，是在前头。

国王在前头往后看了看张大明离他有多么远。还对着张大明笑了笑。

当然这是国王不对。可是那个时候张大明没有工夫想谁对谁不对。他就想叫他的马快快地跑。别的事情就都忘了。

他们刚一跑的时候，张大明的白马在后头，可是离国王的黑马不远。张大明心里很着急，后来他想，美真说她做的马比什么马跑得都快。所以他不着急了。因为他想一会儿他的马一定可以跑到国王的前头去。

在路边儿上，有很多人看。他们都是张大明的朋友。他们看见张大明的白马在后头都很着急。有的人大声地跟张大明说，「快跑！快跑！」也有的人替张大明用力。还有的人大声地叫，谁都不知道他们叫的是什么。

张大明跟国王跑到河边儿上，又跑回来，跑回来的时候，国王的黑马还是在前头。这个时候国王很高兴。可是看的人，都更着急了。这个时候，不但张大明的朋友都很着急，张大明自己也觉得很奇怪。他想美真说的话，一定错不了，可是已经快跑完了，为什么这个马还不跑到前头去呢？他心里跟那个马说，「马先生，马大哥，快跑吧，快跑到前头去吧。再不跑到前头去，就坏了。」那个马真懂他的意思，立刻就跑得快极了。很快地就跑到前头去了。这个时候，看的人都高兴了。

张大明跟国王赛马，最后是张大明先到的。

张大明到了以后，他就放心了，他的朋友也都过来要跟他说话。

他们还没说话呢，这个时候，国王也到了。当然他很生气。下了马就跟张大明说，「今天我的马有病。跑不快，所以你先到了。」

张大明没说什么，可是心里想，「跑马我先到了。那么现在应当没事了吧。」

可是没想到，国王又说，「今天我的马有病，当然不算。」张大明一听，心里说，「坏了。事情还没完。」国王又说，「明天我要跟你赛船。你用你的船，我用我的船。明天早上我跟你在前头那条河里赛。看看谁的船快。要是你没有我快，还是不行，你的太太，美真还是得到我这儿来。」他说完了，带着他手下的人跟马就走了。

张大明站在那个地方想他应当怎么办。这个时候他的朋友都过来问他国王说什么了。他把国王要跟他赛船的话告诉他们了，当然那些人都觉得国王不对。都说他不应当说了话不算。可是张大明说，「有什么法子呢？」那些人有的说这个有的说那个，可是没有人有什么好法子。

张大明说，「多谢多谢。我得回去了。」他就回家了。

Chapter 5 Vocabulary

赛	sài	*V*	*compete*
赛马	sài mǎ	*VP (VO)*	*race horses*
骑	qí	*V*	*ride astride (e.g., on a horse or bicycle)*
铺子	pùzi	*N*	*store*
骑得住	qídezhù	*RV*	*ride and be able to stay on*
活	huó	*V*	*alive*
活了	huó le	*V + le*	*become alive*
河	hé	*N*	*river*
河边(儿)	hébiān (hébiār)	*N*	*riverside*
刚一	gāng yī	*ADV*	*just started to, be about to*
大声地	dà shēng de	*ADV P*	*loudly*
用力	yòng lì	*VP (VO)*	*use one's strength*
大哥	dà gē	*N*	*elder brother (a polite form of address)*
算	suàn	*V*	*count*
不算	bù suàn	*NEG + V*	*does not count*
船	chuán	*N*	*boat*

Chapter 5 Narrative Practice

Summarize the story by translating these sentences into Chinese. Use the parenthesized expressions in your translation.

1. Mr. Gao painted a picture for Zhang Daming. (给)

2. On the picture was a beautiful woman. (上)

3. One day, the woman came down to cook. (下来)

4. The food that she cooked was extremely delicious. (极了)

5. Because she was very pretty, Mr. Gao called her Meizhen. (因为)

6. One day, Meizhen heard two men crying outside. (在外头)

7. She said to the men, "Don't cry anymore." (别)

8. She made two pigeons for them. (给)

9. After the King ate the pigeons, he wanted to see Meizhen. (以后)

10. But Meizhen did not go to see the King. (没)

Chapter 5 Reading Comprehension Questions

Answer the following questions in complete Chinese sentences based on the story.

1. 张大明为什么心里很着急？

2. 美真怎么把纸的马变成真的马？

3. 美真去看张大明赛马吗？为什么？

4. 国王赛马的时候做了什么不对的事？

5. 国王为什么要跟张大明赛船？

第六章：赛船

张大明回到家里，要把那天的事情告诉美真，他还没说呢，美真已经知道了。美真就说，「国王太不对了，我们得想法子。现在我们没有工夫说话，我们得快一点儿做船，船不太容易做。」

张大明不知道美真是怎么知道的。心里觉得奇怪，可是他也没问。他说，「做船得用什么样儿的纸？」

美真说，「做船用纸不行。」

张大明不知道为什么用纸不行。他想，美真用纸做的鸽子，吹一口气就会飞，用纸做的马，吹一口气就会跑，要是用纸做船，吹一口气，不是船也能自己在水里走吗？他这样想，可是没问。他等美真叫他做什么，他就去做。

美真说，「你去找点儿木头来，我们快一点儿做船吧。」

张大明问明白美真要什么样儿的木头，就到外头去找，一会儿的工夫，他就找着了好些，拿回家来了。

张大明没做过船，他一点儿都不知道应当怎么做。他们做船的时候，所有的事情都得美真告诉他。他学得很快，做得也很快。

美真说，「这个船的后头，得做得又尖又硬。」

张大明不懂为什么，可是他知道美真的话一定对。所以他也没问。他就把船的后头做得又尖又硬。

张大明跟美真，两个人都一夜没睡觉，把船做完了。做得很好。他们请朋友帮着他们，把船拿到河边儿上去，放在河里。

张大明一夜没睡觉，也没吃东西，一点精神也没有。美真明白他为什么没精神。也没跟他说什么。就对着他吹了一口气，张大明的精神立刻就来了。

他们看见国王跟他手下的人都来了。美真不愿意见他，就先回家了。

那条河的河边儿上，站着很多人看。张大明的朋友都很着急。因为他们想也许张大明的船比国王的快，可是谁知道以后国王又要跟张大明赛什么呢？

国王到了以后，他们说好了最后到什么地方。他们就上船了。

那个时候，张大明什么都不想，什么都不怕，就划他的船。他的船很快，所以他的船一直地在前头。他的朋友都很高兴。

可是国王的船也不慢，在张大明的船后头，离得很近。

不大的工夫，国王的船走得快极了。那个时候，看的人都觉得很奇怪。他们想要是现在走得那么快，等到快到的时候，他一定就没有气力了。张大明没这样想，张大明知道国王的船离他很近了。他就划得更快了。那个时候两条船走得都很快。

国王的心里，想了一个特别的法子。他想的跟别人想的都不一样。他把船划得那么快，不是要到张大明的前头去，是要碰在张大明的船上，把他的船碰坏了。张大明就一定掉在河里了。那么美真就可以是他的了。

可是他没想到，张大明的船，后头又尖又硬。他的船头碰在张大明的船上的时候，张大明的船没坏，可是把他自己的船头碰坏了。张大明没掉在河里，他自己掉在河里了。

国王在水里上来下去，喝了不少的水。有时候，头在水外头，就大叫。有时候，一个字还没叫出来呢，头又到水里头去了。头在水里就得喝水。喝水喝得太多了，也不知道是应当往东还是应当往西。看人也看不见，找人也找不着。

张大明看见国王掉在河里，他立刻把船划过去，想把国王拉上来。可是那个时候国王手下的人也都到河里去拉他去了。他们七八个人都要把国王拉上来。他们一块儿去拉，有的拉他的手，有的拉他的衣裳，有的往东边儿拉，有的往西边儿拉。拉了半天，他们还是都在河里头。那些拉他的人也都一样地在河里喝水。一样地大叫。

这个时候，张大明看见那些人都没用，他在船上跟那些人说，「你们去吧，我来拉他。」他说着就下去，在水里用手拉住国王后头的衣裳，把他拉到河边儿上去了。

国王那个时候，喝水喝得太多了。差不多什么都不知道了。

过了十几分钟，国王可以站起来了。可是他不知道是谁把他拉上来的。当然他很生气。

他手下的人都不知道说什么好，因为他们不知道国王想什么。他们怕国王说他们做船做得不好，又怕他说他们拉他拉得太慢。可是没想到国王没说那些事情。

国王看看他的衣裳，跟张大明说，「你看，你把我的衣裳弄坏了。这件是我最好的衣裳。三天以后，我打算穿这件衣裳见几个外国客人，你把我的衣裳弄坏了，我那天穿什么？」

他又说，「你快一点儿叫你太太给我做一件新的。跟这件一样。要用鸟儿的毛做。衣裳上得绣上水，还绣上太阳。三天里头一定得给我做好。要不然我就把你杀了。」

张大明没有法子，就回家了。他在路上想来想去，后来他想美真什么都会做，她一定有法子。所以他心里一点儿都不怕，可是他想不出来美真有什么法子。

张大明回到家里，把跟国王赛船的事情告诉美真。美真没等他问做衣裳怎么做，就跟大明说，「三天的工夫太短，我们得快一点儿做。」

张大明帮着美真做过很多事，可是每次做的事都不一样。所以他问美真，「你说我们先做什么？」

美真拿出很多白纸来，跟大明说，「你帮我用这些纸做些个鸟儿。」张大明说，「做什么样儿的鸟儿呢？」美真说，「什么样儿的鸟儿都行。可是有一件事，你得记在心里。就是，你做的时候，心里要想，这些鸟儿，都是我们的朋友，我们有事情，他们都愿意帮我们的忙。」

Chapter 6 Vocabulary

木头	mùtou	*N*	*wood*
尖	jiān	*AV*	*sharp*
硬	yìng	*AV*	*hard, firm*
精神	jīngshén	*N*	*energy*
划船	huá chuán	*VP (VO)*	*row (a) boat*
气力	qìlì	*N*	*strength, energy*
碰	pèng	*V*	*bump (into something)*
掉	diào	*V*	*fall*
弄	nòng	*V*	*make, do*
弄坏	nònghuài	*RV*	*ruin*
新	xīn	*AV*	*new*
鸟(儿)	niǎo(r)	*N*	*bird*
毛	máo	*N*	*feather*
绣	xiù	*V*	*embroider*
太阳	tàiyáng	*N*	*sun*
要不然	yàobùrán	*C*	*otherwise*
短	duǎn	*AV*	*short*
记	jì	*V*	*remember, record*
记在心里	jì zài xīn lǐ	*V + PP*	*record in your heart, keep in mind*

Chapter 6 Structure Notes

6.1. 又 yòu AV_1 又 yòu AV_2 *both AV_1 and AV_2*

To express the meaning *both … and …*, put 又 yòu before each of a series of adjectival verbs.

> 美真说，「这个船的后头，得做得又尖又硬。」
> Měizhēn shuō,「zhège chuán de hòutou, děi zuò de yòu jiān yòu yìng.」
> *Meizhen said, "You have to make the back of this boat both sharp and hard."*

6.2. 又 yòu Action Verb 了 le *did the action again*

To indicate that *an action happened again in the past*, put 又 yòu before the verb phrase that includes the action verb. If the verb phrase begins with a prepositional phrase, put 又 yòu before the prepositional phrase. 了 le generally occurs after the action verb or at the end of the sentence.

> 有一天他又忘了做饭了。
> Yǒu yī tiān tā yòu wàng le zuò fàn le.
> *One day he forgot to cook again.*

> 国王又跟张大明赛船了。
> Guówáng yòu gēn Zhāng Dàmíng sài chuán le.
> *The king raced boats again with Zhang Daming.*

Chapter 6 Structure Exercises

Using the Chapter 6 *Structure Notes* as your guide, translate these English sentences to Chinese.

6.1. 又 yòu AV_1 又 yòu AV_2 *both AV_1 and AV_2*

1. Meizhen cooks food both fast and well.

2. The King was both tall and big. Of course everyone was afraid of him!

6.2. 又 yòu Action Verb 了 le *did the action again*

1. Meizhen made paper pigeons again.

2. The king bumped into Zhang Daming's boat again.

3. The King got angry again.

Chapter 6 Narrative Practice

Write an essay in which you explain what happened during the boat race. Use the following structures and vocabulary in your narrative:

的时候 de shíhou	*(Chapter 1, Structure 1.3)*
Expressing *any*, *every*, *all*, *never*, and *no (noun)*	*(Chapter 1, Structure 1.5)*
把 bǎ	*(Chapter 1, Structure 1.7)*
Resultative Verbs	*(Chapter 2, Structure 2.2)*
Person as Location	*(Chapter 4, Structure 4.2)*
又 yòu AV_1 又 yòu AV_2	*(Chapter 6, Structure 6.1)*

Chapter 6 Reading Comprehension Questions

Answer the following questions in complete Chinese sentences based on the story.

1. 张大明把船的后头做得怎么样？

2. 国王为什么把他的船划得那么快？

3. 国王为什么掉在河里了？

4. 国王要美真做什么样的衣裳？

5. 做鸟儿的时候美真叫张大明想什么？

第七章：做衣裳

大明听了，就立刻帮着美真用纸做鸟儿。做的时候，心里老想着美真告诉他的话，他老想着，这些鸟儿，都是他们的好朋友。一定能帮他们的忙。可是他不知道那些鸟儿怎么能帮着他们。

他们做得很快，一会儿的工夫，就做了很多很多的鸟儿。大的，小的，都有。

他们做完了的时候，那些纸鸟儿，有的在桌子上，有的在地上。张大明看了看，心里想，这些纸鸟儿怎么能帮着做衣裳呢？可是又想美真的法子很多，没有人能知道美真的法子是什么。要是问她，她也不一定说。那么就等着看好了。

他想到这个地方，就看见美真把那些鸟儿用两个手拿起来，往天上一扔，又吹了一口气，那些鸟儿就都飞起来了。这样儿的事情，张大明已经看见过好几次了。所以他也不觉得奇怪了。

那些鸟儿，有的大，有的小，有的飞得很高，有的飞得不太高，可是都很好看。

那些鸟儿在大明跟美真的头上来回地飞，大声地叫。真跟他们的朋友一样。

大明跟美真两个人往上看，看看这个，看看那个。他们真觉得那些鸟儿喜欢他们，他们也真喜欢那些鸟儿。

一会儿有的鸟儿落在张大明的头上，有的落在美真的手上，这个飞走了，那个又来了。他们好像有很多话要说。

那些鸟儿好像都明白，美真跟大明有难办的事，他们都要帮他们两个人的忙，又好像不一定知道得怎么帮他们。所以在他们两个人的头上来回地飞，大声地叫。

后来美真对着那些鸟儿唱了一个歌儿。她唱的是：

「飞，飞，飞！飞到天上去。
飞到天边去。
什么地方好，
就飞到什么地方去。

「看！天多么高！路多么远。
　快快飞！飞吧！飞吧！
　　　　现在天还不太晚。
「飞！飞！快飞！
　飞到什么地方？
　最好是哪儿好，就飞到哪儿。
　可是离开我们以前，
　请把你们的毛给我们一点儿。」
她唱得很好听。

那些鸟儿听美真唱完了歌儿以后，又来回地飞了一会儿，每一个鸟儿都送给他们一点儿毛。因为鸟儿很多，所以毛也很多。那些毛什么颜色都有，从天上飞下来，好看极了。

那些鸟儿都不愿意离开他们两个人，飞走以前都回过头来，看看他们，想要跟他们两个人说，「再见。」

美真看见那些飞着的鸟儿毛，有长的，有短的；颜色都不一样。飞得那么好看，心里很高兴。脸上也带着笑的样子，站在那儿想用手去拿那些飞着的鸟儿毛。那个时候，她把所有的不高兴的事都忘了。

鸟儿的毛一点儿一点儿地落下来，掉在地上。地上的毛很多，可是这边一点儿，那边一点儿，不在一个地方。大明把那些毛放在一块儿，问美真说，「现在我们应当怎么办呢？」美真正看那些鸟儿的毛看得高兴，把所有的事都忘了。听见大明一问，这才想起来，他们的时候不多。做一件那样的衣裳，三天的工夫也许不够。他们得快一点儿去做。所以她跟大明说，「对不起！我忘了我们得做事了。我得立刻去预备。请你立刻把这些鸟儿毛给我拿到房子前头来。」她说完了，就去预备去了。

美真到屋子里去预备她的东西。把她的纺车拿出来，放在他们的房子前头。等大明把鸟儿毛拿来，她就可以纺线。

做那样一件衣裳，很不容易。从纺线到做完了，得经过很多的事情。每一件事情都得用手做。这样儿的事，张大明一点儿都不会。都是美真一个人自己做。大明就能站在那儿看着。帮不了多少忙，最多，就能帮着拿拿东西。

美真知道时候很短，那件衣裳，三天的工夫，不一定做得完。可是她一点儿也不着急。一点儿一点儿地做。因为她知道要是一着急，做错了，就还得再做一次，那样儿，就更慢了。所以她不忙，慢慢地做，可是做得很对。一点儿错的地方都没有。

她三天三夜没睡觉，也没吃饭。

张大明自己知道帮不了什么忙，又知道时候不够。所以他很着急。在那三天三夜里头，他看美真不睡觉，不吃饭，就更着急了。一会儿问问美真吃东西不吃，一会儿又问喝水不喝。他自己，睡觉也睡不着，吃东西也吃不下去。坐着也不好，站着也不好。心里很难过。

美真因为做衣裳，三天三夜没吃东西，也没睡觉；大明因为着急，三天三夜的工夫，吃东西吃不下去，睡觉睡不着。到了第三夜的后半夜，那件衣裳是做完了，可是衣裳上头的水，跟太阳还都没做好。

做衣裳不太难，可是衣裳上头的水跟太阳，很不容易做。因为是不能用笔画，得用线绣。要把太阳跟水绣在衣裳上，不是几个钟头就能绣完的。

美真看看天不早了。再过几个钟头就得把衣裳给国王送去了。这个时候她也有一点儿着急了。

大明睡觉睡不着，就起来站在那儿，看着美真。

美真跟他说，「水跟太阳也许做不完了，这怎么办呢？」

美真没说过「怎么办」。因为每次有事，她都有法子办，这次她一说「怎么办呢？」大明听见以后，心里又着急又难过。不知不觉地就哭起来了。眼泪掉在衣裳上，立刻就变成了绣出来的水的样子。他看见眼泪在衣裳上变成了绣出来的水的样子。觉得很奇怪，立刻就不哭了。后来他想了一会儿，他想什么东西掉在衣裳上，能变成太阳呢？

张大明的眼泪，掉在衣裳上，变成了水的样子。衣裳上的水，看着跟绣上的一样。衣裳上的水有了，可是太阳还是没有。

那时候，天已经快亮了。天一亮，太阳一出来，他们就得把衣裳给国王送去。

可是美真不能把天上的太阳放在衣裳上。因为要是把天上的太阳拿下来，天上就没有太阳了。天上没有太阳，那不是哪儿都是黑的么？那就什么都看不见了。当然美真不能做那样儿的事情。

大明站在那儿想，想了半天还是一点儿法子也没有。他想用笔画一个太阳。他跟美真说，「我在衣裳上画一个太阳行不行？」美真说，「不行。第一，我们没有颜色；第二，画的跟绣的不一样。画在衣裳上，一定不好看。」大明说，「那么怎么办呢？」

那个时候，美真看了看她自己的手，她的手因为做事做得太多了，出了好些血。她就把血放在衣裳上，那些血立刻就变成了一个太阳。

张大明看见美真手上有很多血，他很着急。就问美真说，「你的手怎么样？」美真说，「别着急，不要紧，一会儿就好了。」

Chapter 7 Vocabulary

扔	rēng	*V*	*throw*
落	luò	*V*	*land on, go down*
好像	hǎoxiàng	*V*	*seems as if*
颜色	yánsè	*N*	*color*
回头	huí tóu	*VP (VO)*	*turn one's head*
落下来	luòxialai	*V + DIR*	*come down, descend*
预备	yùbèi	*V*	*prepare*
纺车	fǎng chē	*NP*	*spinning wheel*
线	xiàn	*N*	*thread*
纺线	fǎng xiàn	*VP (VO)*	*spin thread*
难过	nánguò	*AV*	*unhappy*
后半夜	hòu bànyè	*N*	*after midnight (the latter half of the night)*
眼泪	yǎnlèi	*N*	*tears*
亮	liàng	*AV*	*bright*
血	xuè, xiě	*N*	*blood*

Chapter 7 Narrative Practice

Write an essay in which you explain how Meizhen made the thread for the King's new clothing.

In your essay, answer the following questions:

1. What did Meizhen and Zhang Daming do first?

2. Why did they do this?

3. What did they have to think while they were making the birds?

4. Afterwards, how did these paper birds become real birds?

5. How did Meizhen get the birds to give them some of their feathers?

6. How did Meizhen use the feathers?

Use the following expressions in your essay:

Prepositions	*(Chapter 1, Structure 1.4)*
把 bǎ	*(Chapter 1, Structure 1.7)*
因为 yīnweì … 所以 suóyǐ	*(Chapter 3, Structure 3.2)*
的時候 de shíhou	*(Chapter 3, Structure 1.3)*
VP_1 才 cái VP_2	*(Chapter 2, Structure 2.6)*

Chapter 7 Reading Comprehension Questions

Answer the following questions in complete Chinese sentences based on the story.

1. 美真唱的歌是什么意思？

2. 鸟飞走以前都做了什么？

3. 这件衣裳为什么很难做？

4. 美真最后用了什么做衣裳上的太阳？

第八章：送衣裳

衣裳上的水跟太阳都有了。张大明跟美真把那件衣裳放在桌子上，两个人看了半天，他们都觉得那件衣裳好看极了。所以他们心里都很高兴。

当然，张大明心里想，是把衣裳送去以后，就没事了呢？还是国王又叫他们做别的事呢？要是国王老找事情叫他们做，他们应当怎么办？是老给他做呢？还是不给他做了呢？要是不给他做了，他能怎么样呢？他这样想，可是心里不怕，因为他知道，美真一定知道应当怎么办。

那个时候太阳还没出来呢。天已经亮了。张大明拿着那件衣裳，就要给国王送去。他刚一出门，就看见一个大官带着几个人到他们家来了。见着大明，那个大官就很生气地说，「这么晚了，怎么还没把衣裳送去？国王已经生气了。」他没等大明说话，就把衣裳拿过来，叫他手下的人，把大明捆起来，拉着就走。

美真看见他们把大明拉走了，她就跟他们一块儿去了。

他们能把大明怎么样呢？国王见着大明要跟他说什么呢？美真跟他们一块儿去，见着国王，她跟国王说什么呢？

那个大官拿着衣裳，他手下的人，拉着大明去见国王，美真也去了。

那个大官把衣裳给国王看。可是国王看见美真来了，就不想看衣裳了。也不生气了。就笑着跟美真说，「你来了，好极了。」美真说，「你们为什么把张大明捆起来？快一点儿把他放开。」国王看看那个大官，大声地跟他说，「为什么把他捆起来？快一点儿把他放开。」他们就把他放开了。

国王心里还是想不叫美真回去。他就跟美真说，「这件衣裳，做得这么好，真是你做的吗？你得再给我做一件。得在我这儿做，我要看看你怎么做。」

美真说，「这件衣裳，你还没看呢，怎么知道做得好？你得知道，做这件衣裳，很不容易。我用了三天三夜的工夫，没睡觉，也没吃饭，两个手出了很多血，才把你这件衣裳做好。你也不穿上看看，就要叫我再做一件。我告诉你吧！你叫我再做十件都可以，可是你得把这件衣裳穿上给我们看看。」

国王听她说完了，就笑着说，「好！好！我到后头去穿上，给你们看看。你们在这儿等着，别走。」美真说「好。」

张大明心里很生气，又不知道美真心里想什么。更不明白为什么美真要等着看国王穿那件衣裳。

国王到后头去穿新衣裳的时候，才把那件衣裳从上到下看了一看。他看那件衣裳，样子，颜色，上头绣的太阳，绣的水没有一点儿不好。心里高兴极了。他又想，这么大的一件衣裳，每一个地方都是美真用手做的。每一个地方美真的手都拿过。现在，这件美真用自己的手做的衣裳，我要穿了。

他又想，这件衣裳，是美真自己做的。当然，她自己一定喜欢。我穿上这件她喜欢的衣裳，当然她一定也喜欢我。想到这个地方，他自己也不知道他自己有多么的高兴了。

他从后头一出来，因为穿着那么好看的衣裳，不但所有的大官都看他，张大明跟美真也都回过头来，看着他。那些大官都说，「好看极了。」

国王不知道他们说的是「他」好看，是「衣裳」好看，还是「他穿着那件衣裳」好看，可是他觉得那不要紧，他听见那些大官都说，「好看」，他心里比什么都高兴。

美真说，「你过来，我看看。」

他就笑着走过去说，「谢谢你。」一句话还没说完，美真对着衣裳上的水吹了一口气，那些水立刻就变成真水了。

这个时候，美真拉着大明，就出去了。

水从国王的衣裳上出来，出来得很快。不大的工夫，屋子里的地下，都是水。

国王一看，觉得奇怪极了。没有工夫想应当怎么办。那些大官也都不知道怎么办好。他们都很着急。

水越来越多，越来越高。

国王后来想了一个法子，他想他得到高的地方去，他就到桌子上去了。

可是没想到，水是越来越高，他刚一上桌子，水比桌子还高了。他又立刻下了桌子，在水里往外跑。那些大官也跟他一块儿往屋子外头跑。他们想跑到外头去，也许水就没有那么高了。可是他们没想到，他们到什么地方，水就到什么地方。什么地方都是水，水还是越来越高。

一会儿的工夫，水比他们的头还高。他们都在水里上来下去。都大声地叫。可是叫也没用。

美真跟大明出去以后，就到后头屋子，把所有的国王的妃子带到一个小山上去，告诉她们说，「现在国王没有了，大官也没有了，你们可以自由了。你们愿意到什么地方去，就到什么地方。」他们把那些女的带到水边儿上。那个时候，太阳已经出来了。很亮，很好看。美真叫她们看着太阳，跟她们说，「你们的前途，跟太阳一样得光明。」

那些女的走了以后，<u>张大明</u>跟<u>美真</u>，往天上一看，看见他们做的那些鸟儿，都回来看他们。在他们的头上来回地飞，好像给他们唱歌儿，唱的好像是：

黑暗过去。
大放光明。
欢喜快乐。
天下太平。

Chapter 8 Vocabulary

捆	kǔn	*V*	*tie*
捆起来	kǔnqilai	*V + DIR*	*tie up*
放开	fàngkāi	*RV*	*release*
越来越	yuè lái yuè	*INT*	*more and more*
自由	zìyóu	*AV*	*free*
前途	qiántú	*N*	*future*
光明	guāngmíng	*AV*	*bright*
黑暗	hēi'àn	*N*	*darkness*
大放	dà fàng	*VP*	*spread widely*
大放光明	dà fàng guāngmíng	*S*	*brightness is spread widely*
欢喜	huānxǐ	*AV*	*happy, joyous*
快乐	kuàilè	*AV*	*happy*
天下	tiān xià	*N + DIR*	*(all) under heaven*
太平	tàipíng	*AVP*	*(is) at peace*

Chapter 8 Structure Notes

8.1 越来越 AV yuè lái yuè AV *more and more AV*

越来越 yuè lái yuè occurs before an adjectival verb and indicates change over time: *more and more adjectival verb.*

> 水越来越多，越来越高。
> Shuǐ yuè lái yuè duō, yuè lái yuè gāo.
> *There was more and more water and it was higher and higher.*
> *(literally: The water was more and more plentiful, more and more high.)*

A more natural translation for this phrase in English may include the comparative form of the adjective (*higher* instead of *more high*).

When the Mandarin adjectival verb is 多 duō *many* or 少 shǎo *few*, a more natural English translation is usually *there were more/there were fewer.*

The English equivalent of this expression may involve the verb *get* (*the water got higher and higher)* or *become* (*Meizhen became busier and busier*).

Chapter 8 Structure Exercises

Using the Chapter 8 *Structure Notes* as your guide, translate these sentence into Chinese.

8.1 越来越 AV yuè lái yuè AV *more and more AV*

1. The king's horse got faster and faster.

2. Meizhen became more and more anxious.

3. Zhang Daming got sadder and sadder.

Chapter 8 Narrative Practice

Write an essay in which you explain what happened when the King tried on the clothing.

In your essay, answer the following questions:

1. Why didn't Meizhen like the King?

2. Why did she know that the King would be willing to try on the clothing?

3. After the king tried on the clothing, what did Meizhen do?

4. What happened then?

5. What did the King do in the water?

6. Why wasn't the King able to escape?

Use the following structures in your essay:

Prepositions	*(Chapter 1, Structure 1.4)*
把 bǎ	*(Chapter 1, Structure 1.7)*
因为 yīnweì . . . 所以 suóyǐ	*(Chapter 3, Structure 3.2)*
要不然 yàobùrán	*(Chapter 3, Structure 3.2)*
又 yòu AV_1 又 yòu AV_2	*(Chapter 6, Structure 6.1)*
越来越 yuèláiyuè	*(Chapter 8, Structure 8.1)*

Chapter 8 Reading Comprehension Questions

Answer the following questions in complete Chinese sentences based on the story.

1. 衣裳做好了以后张大明还很着急。为什么？

2. 大官为什么把张大明捆起来了？

3. 国王叫美真再给他做一件衣裳。美真听了这话就生气了。为什么？

4. 美真为什么对衣裳上的水吹了一口气？

Vocabulary Index: English - Chinese

	pinyin	simplified characters	traditional characters	grammatical category	chapter
a good many	hǎoxiē	好些	好些	*AVP*	*(2)*
a lot	bù shǎo	不少	不少	*AVP*	*(1)*
ability	běnshi	本事	本事	*N*	*(3)*
about to	gāng yī	刚一	剛一	*ADV*	*(5)*
after midnight	hòu bànyè	后半夜	後半夜	*N*	*(7)*
afterwards	hòulái	后来	後來	*ADV*	*(1)*
alive	huó	活	活	*V*	*(5)*
always	lǎo (shì)	老(是)	老(是)	*ADV*	*(2)*
angry	shēng qì	生气	生氣	*VP (VO)*	*(3)*
anxious	zháojí	着急	着急	*AV*	*(2)*
at peace	tàipíng	太平	太平	*AVP*	*(8)*
back and forth	lái huí	来回	來回	*V + V*	*(4)*
begin to fly	fēiqilai	飞起来	飛起來	*V + DIR*	*(4)*
believe	xìn	信	信	*V*	*(2)*
beneath	dǐxià	底下	底下	*LOC N*	*(2)*
bird	niǎo(r)	鸟(儿)	鳥(兒)	*N*	*(6)*
blood	xuè, xiě	血	血	*N*	*(7)*
blow	chuī	吹	吹	*V*	*(3)*
boat	chuán	船	船	*N*	*(5)*
bow	bài	拜	拜	*V*	*(2)*
bow to heaven and earth	bài tiān bài dì	拜天拜地	拜天拜地	*VO, VO*	*(2)*
box	xiāngzi	箱子	箱子	*N*	*(2)*
bright	guāngmíng	光明	光明	*AV*	*(8)*
bright	liàng	亮	亮	*AV*	*(7)*
brightness is spread widely	dàfàng guāngmíng	大放光明	大放光明	*S*	*(8)*
broken	huài	坏	壞	*AV*	*(1)*
bump	pèng	碰	碰	*V*	*(6)*
burn	zháo	着	着	*V*	*(1)*
call (someone something)	jiào	叫	叫	*V*	*(1)*
call at the door	jiào mén	叫门	叫門	*VP (VO)*	*(4)*
can't go wrong	cuòbuliǎo	错不了	錯不了	*RV*	*(4)*

catch	dǎi	逮	逮	*V*	*(3)*
catch on fire	zháo huǒ	着火	着火	*VP (VO)*	*(1)*
cause	jiào	叫	叫	*V*	*(1)*
change into	biànchéng	变成	變成	*V*	*(3)*
child	háizi	孩子	孩子	*N*	*(1)*
clothing	yīshang	衣裳	衣裳	*N*	*(1)*
color	yánsè	颜色	顏色	*N*	*(7)*
come down	xiàlai	下来	下來	*V (V + DIR)*	*(1)*
come down, descend	luòxialai	落下来	落下來	*V + DIR*	*(7)*
compete	sài	赛	賽	*V*	*(5)*
concubine	fēizi	妃子	妃子	*N*	*(4)*
count	suàn	算	算	*V*	*(5)*
country bumpkin	xiāngxia rén	乡下人	鄉下人	*N*	*(4)*
countryside	xiāngxia	乡下	鄉下	*N*	*(4)*
cry	kū	哭	哭	*V*	*(3)*
darkness	hēi'àn	黑暗	黑暗	*N*	*(8)*
descend	luòxialai	落下来	落下來	*V + DIR*	*(7)*
despicable	bù shi dōngxi	不是东西	不是東西	*VP*	*(4)*
died	guòqule	过去了	過去了	*V*	*(1)*
do	nòng	弄	弄	*V*	*(6)*
do work	bàn shì	办事	辦事	*VP (VO)*	*(4)*
do work	zuò gōng	做工	做工	*VP (VO)*	*(1)*
doctor	dàifu	大夫	大夫	*N*	*(1)*
does not count	bù suàn	不算	不算	*NEG + V*	*(5)*
don't	bié	别	別	*NEG*	*(1)*
don't have to	bú bì	不必	不必	*MVP*	*(3)*
don't have to	bú yòng	不用	不用	*MVP*	*(3)*
drink	hē	喝	喝	*V*	*(3)*
elder brother	dà gē	大哥	大哥	*N*	*(5)*
embarrassed	bù hǎo yìsi	不好意思	不好意思	*AVP*	*(2)*
embroider	xiù	绣	繡	*V*	*(6)*
energy	jīngshén	精神	精神	*N*	*(6)*
energy	qìlì	气力	氣力	*N*	*(6)*
enter (go in)	jìnqu	进去	進去	*V + DIR*	*(1)*
especially	tèbié	特别	特別	*INT*	*(3)*
evening	wǎnshang	晚上	晚上	*N*	*(1)*
excited	zháojí	着急	着急	*AV*	*(2)*

face	liǎn	脸	臉	*N*	*(2)*
fall	diào	掉	掉	*V*	*(6)*
famous	yǒu míng	有名	有名	*AVP*	*(1)*
father	fùqin	父亲	父親	*N*	*(1)*
fear	pà	怕	怕	*V*	*(1)*
feather	máo	毛	毛	*N*	*(6)*
feel	juéde	觉得	覺得	*N*	*(1)*
fire	huǒ	火	火	*N*	*(1)*
firm	yìng	硬	硬	*AV*	*(6)*
for	tì	替	替	*P*	*(4)*
free	zìyóu	自由	自由	*AV*	*(8)*
future	qiántú	前途	前途	*N*	*(8)*
get up	qǐlai	起来	起來	*V + DIR*	*(1)*
go out	chūqu	出去	出去	*V + DIR*	*(1)*
government official	dà guān	大官	大官	*N*	*(3)*
grab hold of	lāzhù	拉住	拉住	*RV*	*(4)*
hair	tóufa	头发	頭髮	*N*	*(2)*
happily	gāogāo xìngxìng de	高高兴兴地	高高興興地	*ADV P*	*(3)*
happy	gāoxìng	高兴	高興	*AV*	*(1)*
happy	kuàilè	快乐	快樂	*AV*	*(8)*
happy	huānxǐ	欢喜	歡喜	*AV*	*(8)*
hard	yìng	硬	硬	*AV*	*(6)*
have fun	wán (wár)	玩(儿)	玩(兒)	*V*	*(1)*
hear	tīngjiàn	听见	聽見	*RV*	*(2)*
help	bāng máng	帮忙	幫忙	*VP (VO)*	*(1)*
help me a bit	bāng wǒ yīdiǎn máng	帮我一点忙	幫我一點忙	*VP*	*(1)*
immediately	lìkè	立刻	立刻	*ADV*	*(1)*
impolitely	bù kèqi de	不客气地	不客氣地	*ADV P*	*(4)*
important	yàojǐn	要紧	要緊	*AV*	*(4)*
in a short time	bù dà de gōngfu	不大的工夫	不大的工夫	*ADV P*	*(1)*
in his heart	xīn lǐ	心里	心裏	*N + LOC*	*(1)*
in the night	yè lǐ	夜里	夜裏	*N + LOC*	*(1)*
in the past	cóngqián	从前	從前	*ADV*	*(1)*
inform	gàosu	告诉	告訴	*V*	*(2)*
interesting	yǒu yìsi	有意思	有意思	*AVP*	*(1)*
involuntarily	bù zhī bù juéde	不知不觉地	不知不覺地	*ADV P*	*(2)*

joyous	huānxǐ	欢喜	歡喜	*AV*	*(8)*
just about to	zhèng yào	正要	正要	*ADV + MV*	*(1)*
just started to	gāng yī	刚一	剛一	*ADV*	*(5)*
keep in mind	jì zài xīn lǐ	记在心里	記在心裏	*V + PP*	*(6)*
kill	shā	杀	殺	*V*	*(3)*
king	guówáng	国王	國王	*N*	*(3)*
kneel	guì	跪	跪	*V*	*(2)*
know (a person)	rènshi	认识	認識	*V*	*(1)*
land	luò	落	落	*V*	*(7)*
landscape	shānshuǐ	山水	山水	*N*	*(1)*
listen	tīng	听	聽	*V*	*(1)*
live (in a place)	zhù	住	住	*V*	*(2)*
long time	bàntiān	半天	半天	*N*	*(4)*
loudly	dà shēng de	大声地	大聲地	*ADV P*	*(5)*
love	ài	爱	愛	*V*	*(1)*
make	nòng	弄	弄	*V*	*(6)*
marry	jiéhūn	结婚	結婚	*V*	*(2)*
mistaken	cuò	错	錯	*AV*	*(4)*
more and more	yuè lái yuè	越来越	越來越	*INT*	*(8)*
morning	zǎoshang	早上	早上	*N*	*(1)*
mother	mǔqin	母亲	母親	*N*	*(1)*
must	děi	得	得	*MV*	*(1)*
need not	bú bì	不必	不必	*MVP*	*(3)*
need not	bú yòng	不用	不用	*MVP*	*(3)*
new	xīn	新	新	*AV*	*(6)*
not only	búdàn	不但	不但	*C*	*(1)*
of course	dāngrán	当然	當然	*ADV*	*(1)*
often	cháng	常	常	*ADV*	*(1)*
okay	xíng le	行了	行了	*V*	*(3)*
older brother	gēge	哥哥	哥哥	*N*	*(1)*
on behalf of others	tì	替	替	*P*	*(4)*
once upon a time	cóngqián	从前	從前	*ADV*	*(1)*
one mouthful of air	yī kǒu qì	一口气	一口氣	*NP*	*(3)*
oneself	zìjǐ	自己	自己	*PrN*	*(1)*

open	kāi	开	開	*V*	*(1)*
other people	bié rén	别人	別人	*NP*	*(1)*
otherwise	yàobùrán	要不然	要不然	*C*	*(6)*
paint	huà	画	畫	*V*	*(1)*
paint picture(s)	huà huà(r)	画画(儿)	畫畫(兒)	*VP (VO)*	*(1)*
paper	zhǐ	纸	紙	*N*	*(2)*
passed away	guòqule	过去了	過去了	*V*	*(1)*
pay taxes	shàng shuì	上税	上稅	*VP (VO)*	*(3)*
perhaps	yéxǔ	也许	也許	*ADV*	*(1)*
pigeon	gēzi	鸽子	鴿子	*N*	*(3)*
place	dìfang	地方	地方	*N*	*(3)*
plan	fǎzi	法子	法子	*N*	*(2)*
play	wán (wár)	玩(儿)	玩(兒)	*V*	*(1)*
play a joke	kāi wánxiào	开玩笑	開玩笑	*VP (VO)*	*(1)*
pocket	kǒudài (kǒudàr)	口袋(儿)	口袋(兒)	*N*	*(4)*
polite M for people	wèi	位	位	*M*	*(1)*
prepare	yùbèi	预备	預備	*V*	*(7)*
present as a gift	sòng	送	送	*V*	*(1)*
pull	lā	拉	拉	*V*	*(4)*
put down	fàng	放	放	*V*	*(1)*
race horses	sài mǎ	赛马	賽馬	*VP (VO)*	*(5)*
record	jì	记	記	*V*	*(6)*
record in your heart	jì zài xīn lǐ	记在心里	記在心裏	*V + PP*	*(6)*
red	hóng	红	紅	*V*	*(2)*
relax, stop worrying	fàng xīn	放心	放心	*VP (VO)*	*(1)*
release	fàngkāi	放开	放開	*RV*	*(8)*
remember	jì	记	記	*V*	*(6)*
reside	zhù	住	住	*V*	*(2)*
restrain	lazhù	拉住	拉住	*RV*	*(4)*
return (to a place)	huí	回	回	*V*	*(1)*
return home	huí jiā	回家	回家	*VP (VO)*	*(1)*
ride and be able to stay on	qídezhù	骑得住	騎得住	*RV*	*(5)*
ride astride	qí	骑	騎	*V*	*(5)*

right at that moment	zhèng	正	正	*ADV*	*(2)*
river	hé	河	河	*N*	*(5)*
riverside	hébiān (hébiār)	河边(儿)	河邊(兒)	*N*	*(5)*
room	wūzi	屋子	屋子	*N*	*(1)*
row (a) boat	huá chuán	划船	划船	*VP (VO)*	*(6)*
ruin	nònghuài	弄坏	弄壞	*RV*	*(6)*
ruined	huài	坏	壞	*AV*	*(1)*
run	pǎo	跑	跑	*V*	*(1)*
scenery	shānshuǐ	山水	山水	*N*	*(1)*
seems as if	hǎoxiàng	好像	好像	*V*	*(7)*
send	sòng	送	送	*V*	*(1)*
sew	féng	缝	縫	*V*	*(1)*
sharp	jiān	尖	尖	*AV*	*(6)*
short	duǎn	短	短	*AV*	*(6)*
should	yīngdāng	应当	應當	*MV*	*(1)*
sick	bìng	病	病	*V*	*(1)*
sing	chàng	唱	唱	*V*	*(1)*
sing (a) song, sing songs	chàng gē(r)	唱歌(儿)	唱歌(兒)	*VP (VO)*	*(1)*
sit down	zuòxia	坐下	坐下	*V + DIR*	*(1)*
sleep	shuì jiào	睡觉	睡覺	*VP (VO)*	*(1)*
slowly	mànmān de (mànmār de)	慢慢(儿)地	慢慢(兒)地	*ADV P*	*(3)*
smile	xiào	笑	笑	*V*	*(1)*
smoke	yān	烟	煙	*N*	*(1)*
snack	diǎnxīn	点心	點心	*N*	*(1)*
so good to eat	zhème hǎo chī	这么好吃	這麼好吃	*ADV + VP*	*(1)*
solution	fǎzi	法子	法子	*N*	*(2)*
sometimes	yǒu shíhou	有时候	有時候	*ADV*	*(1)*
song, songs	gē(r)	歌(儿)	歌(兒)	*N*	*(1)*
spin thread	fǎng xiàn	纺线	紡線	*VP (VO)*	*(7)*
spinning wheel	fǎng chē	纺车	紡車	*NP*	*(7)*
spirit	jīngshén	精神	精神	*N*	*(6)*
spread widely	dà fàng	大放	大放	*VP*	*(8)*
stand	zhàn	站	站	*V*	*(1)*
store	pùzi	铺子	鋪子	*N*	*(5)*
strange	qíguài	奇怪	奇怪	*AV*	*(1)*
strength	qìlì	气力	氣力	*N*	*(6)*
subordinate	shǒuxià	手下	手下	*N*	*(3)*

suddenly	hūrán	忽然	忽然	*ADV*	*(3)*
sun	tàiyáng	太阳	太陽	*N*	*(6)*
table	zhuōzi	桌子	桌子	*N*	*(1)*
take	ná	拿	拿	*V*	
take along (with them)	dài	带	帶	*V*	*(3)*
talent	běnshi	本事	本事	*N*	*(3)*
talk nonsense	hú shuō	胡说	胡說	*ADV + V*	*(4)*
taxes	shuì	税	税	*N*	*(3)*
tea	chá	茶	茶	*N*	*(3)*
tears	yǎnlèi	眼泪	眼淚	*N*	*(7)*
tell	gàosu	告诉	告訴	*V*	*(2)*
that kind (of)	nàyàng (nàyàr)	那样(儿)	那樣(兒)	*SP + M*	*(2)*
therefore	suóyǐ	所以	所以	*C*	*(1)*
thing (abstract, e.g., work)	shìqing	事情	事情	*N*	*(1)*
thing (concrete)	dōngxi	东西	東西	*N*	*(1)*
think	juéde	觉得	覺得	*V*	*(1)*
think over and over	xiǎnglái xiǎngqù	想来 想去	想來 想去	*V + DIR, V + DIR*	*(1)*
this good to eat	zhème hǎo chī	这么好吃	這麼好吃	*ADV + VP*	*(1)*
this kind of	zhèyàng	这样	這樣	*SP + M*	*(1)*
thread	xiàn	线	線	*N*	*(7)*
throw	rēng	扔	扔	*V*	*(7)*
tie	kǔn	捆	捆	*V*	*(8)*
tie up	kǔnqilai	捆起来	捆起來	*V (V+DIR)*	*(8)*
together	yíkuài (yíkuàr)	一块(儿)	一塊(兒)	*ADV*	*(1)*
torn	huài	坏	壞	*AV*	*(1)*
towards	wǎng	往	往	*P*	*(1)*
trunk	xiāngzi	箱子	箱子	*N*	*(2)*
turn one's head	huí tóu	回头	回頭	*VP (VO)*	*(7)*
unable to be mistaken	cuòbuliǎo	错不了	錯不了	*RV*	*(4)*
unable to fall asleep	shuìbuzháo	睡不着	睡不着	*RV*	*(1)*
under heaven	tiānxià	天下	天下	*N + DIR*	*(8)*
understand	dǒng	懂	懂	*V*	*(3)*

unhappy	nánguò	难过	難過	*AV*	*(7)*
uninteresting	méi yìsi	没意思	沒意思	*NEG + AVP*	*(1)*
use one's strength	yòng lì	用力	用力	*VP (VO)*	*(5)*
usually	píngcháng	平常	平常	*ADV*	*(1)*
wait (until)	děng	等	等	*V*	*(3)*
wear	chuān	穿	穿	*V*	*(2)*
what best to do	zěnme bàn hǎo	怎么办好	怎麼辦好	*VP*	*(2)*
what is going on?	zěnme huí shì?	怎么回事？	怎麼回事？	*Question*	*(1)*
what's the matter?	zěnme le?	怎么了？	怎麼了？	*Question*	*(3)*
willing	yuànyi	愿意	願意	*AV*	*(1)*
window	chuānghu	窗户	窗户	*N*	*(2)*
with	gēn	跟	跟	*P*	*(1)*
wood	mùtou	木头	木頭	*N*	*(6)*
work (do work)	zuò gōng	做工	做工	*VP (VO)*	*(1)*
worship	bài	拜	拜	*V*	*(2)*
wrong	cuò	错	錯	*AV*	*(4)*
years of age	suì	岁	歲	*M*	*(1)*
younger brother	dìdi	弟弟	弟弟	*N*	*(1)*

Vocabulary Index: Chinese (Pinyin) - English

	simplified characters	traditional characters	grammatical category	English	chapter
ài	爱	愛	*V*	*love*	*(1)*
bài	拜	拜	*V*	*bow*	*(2)*
bài tiān bài dì	拜天拜地	拜天拜地	*VO, VO*	*pray to heaven and earth*	*(2)*
bàn shì	办事	辦事	*VP (VO)*	*do work*	*(4)*
bàn tiān	半天	半天	*N*	*for a long time, a half day*	*(4)*
bāng máng	帮忙	幫忙	*VP (VO)*	*help*	*(1)*
bāng wǒ yīdiǎn máng	帮我一点忙	幫我一點忙	*VP*	*help me a bit*	*(1)*
běnshi	本事	本事	*N*	*talent, ability*	*(3)*
biànchéng	变成	變成	*V*	*change into*	*(3)*
bié	别	別	*NEG*	*don't*	*(1)*
bié rén	别人	別人	*NP*	*other people*	*(1)*
bìng	病	病	*V*	*sick*	*(1)*
bú bì	不必	不必	*NEG + MV*	*do not have to*	*(3)*
bù dà de gōngfu	不大的工夫	不大的工夫	*ADV P*	*in a short time*	*(1)*
bú dàn	不但	不但	*C*	*not only*	*(1)*
bù hǎo yìsi	不好意思	不好意思	*AVP*	*embarrassed*	*(2)*
bù kèqi de	不客气地	不客氣地	*ADV P*	*impolitely*	*(4)*
bù shǎo	不少	不少	*AV P*	*a lot, not few*	*(1)*
bù shi dōngxi	不是东西	不是東西	*VP*	*be nothing, be despicable*	*(4)*
bù suàn	不算	不算	*NEG + V*	*does not count*	*(5)*
bú yòng	不用	不用	*NEG + MV*	*do not have to*	*(3)*
bù zhī bù juéde	不知不觉地	不知不覺地	*ADV P*	*involuntarily*	*(2)*
chá	茶	茶	*N*	*tea*	*(3)*
cháng	常	常	*ADV*	*often*	*(1)*
chàng	唱	唱	*V*	*sing*	*(1)*
chàng gē(r)	唱歌(儿)	唱歌(兒)	*VP (VO)*	*sing (songs)*	*(1)*
chuān	穿	穿	*V*	*wear*	*(2)*
chuán	船	船	*N*	*boat*	*(5)*
chuānghu	窗户	窗戶	*N*	*window*	*(2)*
chuī	吹	吹	*V*	*blow*	*(3)*
chūqu	出去	出去	*V + DIR*	*go out*	*(1)*
cóngqián	从前	從前	*ADV*	*in the past, once upon a time*	*(1)*
cuò	错	錯	*AV*	*mistaken, wrong*	*(4)*

cuòbuliǎo	错不了	錯不了	*RV*	*unable to be mistaken, can't go wrong*	*(4)*
dà fàng	大放	大放	*VP*	*spread widely*	*(8)*
dà fàng guāngmíng	大放光明	大放光明	*S*	*brightness is spread widely*	*(8)*
dà gē	大哥	大哥	*N*	*elder brother (a polite form of address)*	*(5)*
dà guān	大官	大官	*N*	*government official*	*(3)*
dà shēng de	大声地	大聲地	*ADV P*	*loudly*	*(5)*
dǎi	逮	逮	*V*	*catch*	*(3)*
dài	带	帶	*V*	*take along*	*(3)*
dàifu	大夫	大夫	*N*	*doctor*	*(1)*
dāngrán	当然	當然	*ADV*	*of course*	*(1)*
děi	得	得	*MV*	*must*	*(1)*
děng	等	等	*V*	*wait (until)*	*(3)*
diǎnxīn	点心	點心	*N*	*snack*	*(1)*
diào	掉	掉	*V*	*fall*	*(6)*
dìdi	弟弟	弟弟	*N*	*younger brother*	*(1)*
dìfang	地方	地方	*N*	*place*	*(3)*
dǐxià	底下	底下	*LOC N*	*beneath*	*(2)*
dǒng	懂	懂	*V*	*understand*	*(3)*
dōngxi	东西	東西	*N*	*thing (concrete)*	*(1)*
duǎn	短	短	*AV*	*short*	*(6)*
fàng	放	放	*V*	*put down*	*(1)*
fǎng chē	纺车	紡車	*NP*	*spinning wheel*	*(7)*
fǎng xiàn	纺线	紡線	*VP (VO)*	*spin thread*	*(7)*
fàng xīn	放心	放心	*VP (VO)*	*relax, stop worrying*	*(1)*
fàngkāi	放开	放開	*RV*	*release*	*(8)*
fǎzi	法子	法子	*N*	*plan, solution*	*(2)*
fēiqilai	飞起来	飛起來	*V + DIR*	*begin to fly*	*(4)*
fēizi	妃子	妃子	*N*	*concubine*	*(4)*
féng	缝	縫	*V*	*sew*	*(1)*
fùqin	父亲	父親	*N*	*father*	*(1)*
gāng yī	刚一	剛一	*ADV*	*just started to, be about to*	*(5)*
gāogāo xìngxìng de	高高兴兴地	高高興興地	*ADV P*	*happily*	*(3)*
gàosu	告诉	告訴	*V*	*inform, tell*	*(2)*

gāoxìng	高兴	高興	*AV*	*happy*	*(1)*
gē(r)	歌(儿)	歌(兒)	*N*	*song(s)*	*(1)*
gēge	哥哥	哥哥	*N*	*older brother*	*(1)*
gēn	跟	跟	*P*	*with*	*(1)*
gēzi	鸽子	鴿子	*N*	*pigeon*	*(3)*
guāngmíng	光明	光明	*AV*	*bright*	*(8)*
guì	跪	跪	*V*	*kneel*	*(2)*
guòqule	过去了	過去了	*V*	*passed away (died)*	*(1)*
guówáng	国王	國王	*N*	*king*	*(3)*
háizi	孩子	孩子	*N*	*child*	*(1)*
hǎoxiàng	好像	好像	*V*	*seems as if*	*(7)*
hǎoxiē	好些	好些	*AVP*	*a good many*	*(2)*
hē	喝	喝	*V*	*drink*	*(3)*
hé	河	河	*N*	*river*	*(5)*
hébiān (hébiār)	河边(儿)	河邊(兒)	*N*	*riverside*	*(5)*
hēi'àn	黑暗	黑暗	*N*	*darkness*	*(8)*
hóng	红	紅	*V*	*red*	*(2)*
hòu bànyè	后半夜	後半夜	*N*	*after midnight, the latter half of the night*	*(7)*
hòulái	后来	後來	*ADV*	*afterwards*	*(1)*
hú shuō	胡说	胡說	*ADV + V*	*talk nonsense*	*(4)*
huà	画	畫	*V*	*paint*	*(1)*
huà(r)	画(儿)	畫(兒)	*N*	*painting(s), picture(s)*	*(1)*
huá chuán	划船	划船	*VP (VO)*	*row (a) boat*	*(6)*
huà huà(r)	画画(儿)	畫畫(兒)	*VP (VO)*	*paint picture(s)*	*(1)*
huài	坏	壞	*AV*	*torn, broken, ruined*	*(1)*
huānxǐ	欢喜	歡喜	*AV*	*happy, joyous*	*(8)*
huí	回	回	*V*	*return (to a place)*	*(1)*
huí jiā	回家	回家	*VP (VO)*	*return home*	*(1)*
huí tóu	回头	回頭	*VP (VO)*	*turn one's head*	*(7)*
huǒ	火	火	*N*	*fire*	*(1)*
huó	活	活	*V*	*alive, living*	*(5)*
hūrán	忽然	忽然	*ADV*	*suddenly*	*(3)*
jì	记	記	*V*	*remember, record*	*(6)*
jì zài xīn lǐ	记在心里	記在心裏	*V + PP*	*record in your heart, keep in mind*	*(6)*
jiān	尖	尖	*AV*	*sharp*	*(6)*

jiào	叫	叫	*V*	*cause (someone to do or feel something)*	*(1)*
jiào mén	叫门	叫門	*VP (VO)*	*call at the door*	*(4)*
jiéhūn	结婚	結婚	*V*	*marry*	*(2)*
jīngshén	精神	精神	*N*	*energy*	*(6)*
jìnqu	进去	進去	*V + DIR*	*enter*	*(1)*
juéde	觉得	覺得	*V*	*think, feel*	*(1)*
kāi	开	開	*V*	*open*	*(1)*
kāi wánxiào	开玩笑	開玩笑	*VP (VO)*	*play a joke*	*(1)*
kǒudài (kǒudàr)	口袋(儿)	口袋(兒)	*N*	*pocket*	*(4)*
kū	哭	哭	*V*	*cry*	*(3)*
kuàilè	快乐	快樂	*AV*	*happy*	*(8)*
kǔn	捆	捆	*V*	*tie*	*(8)*
kǔnqilai	捆起来	捆起來	*V+ DIR*	*tie up*	*(8)*
lā	拉	拉	*V*	*pull*	*(4)*
lái huí	来回	來回	*V + V*	*back and forth*	*(4)*
lǎo (shì)	老(是)	老(是)	*ADV*	*always*	*(2)*
lāzhù	拉住	拉住	*RV*	*restrain, grab hold of*	*(4)*
liǎn	脸	臉	*N*	*face*	*(2)*
liàng	亮	亮	*AV*	*bright*	*(7)*
lìkè	立刻	立刻	*ADV*	*immediately*	*(1)*
luò	落	落	*V*	*land*	*(7)*
luòxialai	落下来	落下來	*V + DIR*	*come down, descend*	*(7)*
mànmān de (mànmār de)	慢慢(儿)地	慢慢(兒)地	*ADV P*	*slowly*	*(3)*
máo	毛	毛	*N*	*feather*	*(6)*
méi yìsi	没意思	沒意思	*NEG + AVP*	*not interesting*	*(1)*
mǔqin	母亲	母親	*N*	*mother*	*(1)*
mùtou	木头	木頭	*N*	*wood*	*(6)*
ná	拿	拿	*V*	*take*	*(1)*
nánguò	难过	難過	*AV*	*unhappy*	*(7)*
nàyàng (nàyàr)	那样(儿)	那樣(兒)	*SP + M*	*that kind (of)*	*(2)*
niǎo(r)	鸟(儿)	鳥(兒)	*N*	*bird*	*(6)*
nòng	弄	弄	*V*	*make, do*	*(6)*
nònghuài	弄坏	弄壞	*RV*	*ruin*	*(6)*
pà	怕	怕	*V*	*fear*	*(1)*

pǎo	跑	跑	*V*	*run*	(1)
pèng	碰	碰	*V*	*bump*	(6)
píngcháng	平常	平常	*ADV*	*usually*	(1)
pùzi	铺子	鋪子	*N*	*store*	(5)
qí	骑	騎	*V*	*ride astride (e.g., on a horse or bicycle)*	(5)
qiántú	前途	前途	*N*	*future*	(8)
qídezhù	骑得住	騎得住	*RV*	*ride and be able to stay on*	(5)
qíguài	奇怪	奇怪	*AV*	*strange*	(1)
qǐlai	起来	起來	*V + DIR*	*get up*	(1)
qìlì	气力	氣力	*N*	*strength, energy*	(6)
rēng	扔	扔	*V*	*throw*	(7)
rènshi	认识	認識	*V*	*know (a person)*	(1)
sài	赛	賽	*V*	*compete*	(5)
sài mǎ	赛马	賽馬	*VP (VO)*	*race horses*	(5)
shā	杀	殺	*V*	*kill*	(3)
shàng shuì	上税	上稅	*VP (VO)*	*pay taxes*	(3)
shānshuǐ	山水	山水	*N*	*landscape, scenery*	(1)
shēng qì	生气	生氣	*VP (VO)*	*be angry, become angry*	(3)
shìqing	事情	事情	*N*	*thing (abstract, e.g., work)*	(1)
shǒuxià	手下	手下	*N*	*subordinate*	(3)
shuì	税	稅	*N*	*taxes*	(3)
shuì jiào	睡觉	睡覺	*VP (VO)*	*sleep*	(1)
shuìbuzháo	睡不着	睡不着	*RV*	*unable to fall asleep*	(1)
sòng	送	送	*V*	*send, present as a gift*	(1)
suàn	算	算	*V*	*count*	(5)
suì	岁	歲	*M*	*years of age*	(1)
suóyǐ	所以	所以	*C*	*therefore*	(1)
tàipíng	太平	太平	*VP*	*at peace*	(8)
tàiyáng	太阳	太陽	*N*	*sun*	(6)
tèbié	特别	特別	*INT*	*especially*	(3)
tì	替	替	*P*	*for, on behalf of*	(4)
tiānxià	天下	天下	*N + DIR*	*(all) under heaven*	(8)
tīng	听	聽	*V*	*listen*	(1)
tīngjiàn	听见	聽見	*RV*	*hear*	(2)

tóufa	头发	頭髮	*N*	*hair*	*(2)*
wán (wár)	玩(儿)	玩(兒)	*V*	*have fun, play*	*(1)*
wǎng	往	往	*P*	*towards*	*(1)*
wǎnshang	晚上	晚上	*N*	*evening*	*(1)*
wèi	位	位	*M*	*polite M for people*	*(1)*
wūzi	屋子	屋子	*N*	*room*	*(1)*
xiàlai	下来	下來	*V + DIR*	*come down*	*(1)*
xiàn	线	線	*N*	*thread*	*(7)*
xiǎnglái xiǎngqù	想来 想去	想來 想去	*V + DIR, V + DIR*	*think over and over*	*(1)*
xiāngxia	乡下	鄉下	*N*	*countryside*	*(4)*
xiāngxia rén	乡下人	鄉下人	*N*	*country bumpkin*	*(4)*
xiāngzi	箱子	箱子	*N*	*box, trunk*	*(2)*
xiào	笑	笑	*V*	*smile*	*(1)*
xīn	新	新	*AV*	*new*	*(6)*
xìn	信	信	*V*	*believe*	*(2)*
xīn lǐ	心里	心裏	*N + LOC*	*in his heart*	*(1)*
xíng le	行了	行了	*V*	*okay*	*(3)*
xiù	绣	繡	*V*	*embroider*	*(6)*
xuè, xiě	血	血	*N*	*blood*	*(7)*
yān	烟	煙	*N*	*smoke*	*(1)*
yǎnlèi	眼泪	眼淚	*N*	*tears*	*(7)*
yánsè	颜色	顏色	*N*	*color*	*(7)*
yàobùrán	要不然	要不然	*C*	*otherwise*	*(6)*
yàojǐn	要紧	要緊	*AV*	*important*	*(4)*
yè lǐ	夜里	夜裏	*N + LOC*	*in the night*	*(1)*
yéxǔ	也许	也許	*ADV*	*perhaps*	*(1)*
yī kǒu qì	一口气	一口氣	*NP*	*one mouthful of air*	*(3)*
yíkuài (yíkuàr)	一块(儿)	一塊(兒)	*ADV*	*together*	*(1)*
yìng	硬	硬	*AV*	*hard, firm*	*(6)*
yīngdāng	应当	應當	*MV*	*should*	*(1)*
yīshang	衣裳	衣裳	*N*	*clothing*	*(1)*
yòng lì	用力	用力	*VP (VO)*	*use one's strength*	*(5)*
yǒu míng	有名	有名	*AVP*	*famous*	*(1)*
yǒu shíhou	有时候	有時候	*ADV*	*sometimes*	*(1)*
yǒu yìsi	有意思	有意思	*AVP*	*interesting*	*(1)*
yuànyi	愿意	願意	*AV*	*willing*	*(1)*
yùbèi	预备	預備	*V*	*prepare*	*(7)*

yuè lái yuè	越来越	越來越	*ADV*	*more and more*	*(8)*
zǎoshang	早上	早上	*N*	*morning*	*(1)*
zěnme bàn hǎo	怎么办好	怎麼辦好	*VP*	*what best to do*	*(2)*
zěnme huí shì?	怎么回事？	怎麼回事？	*Question*	*what is going on?*	*(1)*
zěnme le?	怎么了？	怎麼了？	*Question*	*what's the matter?*	*(3)*
zhàn	站	站	*V*	*stand*	*(1)*
zháo	着	着	*V*	*burn*	*(1)*
zháo huǒ	着火	着火	*VP (VO)*	*catch on fire*	*(1)*
zháojí	着急	着急	*AV*	*anxious, excited*	*(2)*
zhème hǎo chī	这么好吃	這麼好吃	*ADV + VP*	*this good to eat, so good to eat*	*(1)*
zhèng	正	正	*ADV*	*right at that moment*	*(2)*
zhèng yào	正要	正要	*ADV + MV*	*be just about to*	*(1)*
zhèyàng	这样	這樣	*SP + M*	*this kind of*	*(1)*
zhǐ	纸	紙	*N*	*paper*	*(2)*
zhù	住	住	*V*	*live (in a place), reside*	*(2)*
zhuōzi	桌子	桌子	*N*	*table*	*(1)*
zìjǐ	自己	自己	*PrN*	*(by) oneself*	*(1)*
zìyóu	自由	自由	*AV*	*free*	*(8)*
zuò gōng	做工	做工	*VP (VO)*	*works (do work)*	*(1)*
zuòxia	坐下	坐下	*V + DIR*	*sit down*	*(1)*

Structure Index